My Common, Remarkable Family

PACKARDS AND ALLENS;
CIVIL WAR TO THE TWENTY FIRST CENTURY

Editor: Tony Allen

Copyright © 2012 Charles A. Allen

All rights reserved.

ISBN: 0985817917
ISBN-13: 9780985817916

DEDICATION

To my remarkable parents, grandparents, and great grandparents who left us the treasure of their memories.

CONTENTS

	Preface	i
1	Georgiana's Story	2
2	Cyrus Packard and Family Letters Before Immigrating	28
3	Georgiana Packard Letters	41
4	George Washington Packard Letters	54
5	Addendum I	97
6	My Reflections by Ruth Packard Allen	109
7	Addendum II	146
8	This Is Me by George	161
9	Addendum III	195
10	Appendix	222
	1. Underground Railroad Stories	223
	2. Packard Genealogy by Georgiana Packard	245
	3. Best Available Genealogy for Ruth Packard	247
	4. Best Available Genealogy for George Allen	256
	5. Handwritten Letter by Georgiana Packard	261
	6. Handwritten Letter by George Washington Packard	265
	7. George W. Packard Civil War Pay Records	268
	About the Author	279

ACKNOWLEDGMENTS

It is a blessing these documents were written and preserved so we can enjoy and understand them. For that we must thank my mother, Ruth Allen, who not only recognized their importance, but spent countless hours deciphering the handwriting and typing them into more readable form. Thanks also to my wife Gloria, granddaughter Challis McNally and Sister-In-Law Vicki Allen for their time and effort in proofreading and editing. Unfortunately I frequently demonstrate the ability to overcome the best proofreading and the errors in this text belong to me.

Tony Allen

Tony Allen

PREFACE

Our ancestral family resembles many American families with truly great people who struggled to provide physical well-being, cultural awareness, and sense of morality to their families. We were blessed to have a record of some of these times recorded as letters or stories. These documents illustrate the mundane and remarkable lives our ancestors led. Many of their understated sentences could easily be the basis for a book.

My great grandmother, Georgiana Packard, documented her move with her family from Maine to Kansas because her father, Cyrus Packard, read Uncle Tom's Cabin and like many New Englanders wanted to help Kansas become a free state. Her story includes life on the Kansas Plains including her marriage to her cousin George Washington Packard who also moved to Kansas from Maine.

My mother, Ruth Packard Allen, found in the family archives letters that my great grandfather wrote home during his service in the Kansas Cavalry for the Union Army and a few letters after he and Georgiana were married. We marvel at his penmanship, but in the modern era few of us could read it well. My mother took on the task of deciphering the letters and typing them. In that way the old letters on deteriorating paper could be enjoyed by future generations.

Following in her grandmother's footsteps, Ruth wrote a short biography of her life through the depression, World War II, and her life with my father George Allen. She references national and international events to add context. Her fascination with fashion comes through, but the focus is on her life with her parents, my father, her children, and grandchildren.

My father grew up the son of a Methodist minister who spent much of his life as Chaplain at Leavenworth Federal Penitentiary. He told many stories of being raised in part by trustee yardmen, Midnight and Ben Long Ear. Mom asked him to write down his stories, but he put it off. During the final year of his life, Mom solved the problem by talking with him about his memories then typed the stories and went over them with Dad.

My wife and I inherited family history photographs from both sides of the family, many dating from the 1800s. Some of these I include to add flavor to the history. I added an Addendum at the end of each of the sections to capture the images of these amazing people. The photo on the front cover is the Veteran's marker on Cyrus Packard's grave in the Rochester Cemetery near Topeka, and the back cover photo of Georgiana is from the studio portrait of the four Packard sisters.

Sharing this information with the Allen/Packard family and other descendants is the sole motivation for editing and publishing this book. I know there is not a broad interest in this slice of history of one family, as most families in the world share fascinating histories.

Tony Allen

My Common, Remarkable Family

1 GEORGIANA'S STORY

Forward

Georgiana Packard married her cousin George Washington Packard in Kansas after they separately emigrated from Maine. Georgiana's family lived near Monson, Maine, in the central part of the state, and George Washington Packard lived in the Hebron area in Southwestern Maine.

Georgiana's father, Cyrus Packard, decided to help Kansas become a free state after reading Uncle Tom's Cabin. Georgiana wrote her story from memory when she was about 70, after her husband's death in 1912. She wrote it so her children could know their heritage. There is some question on the spelling of Georgiana,- one "n" or two, most of the time it appears with one "n" so that is what I went with.

Her autobiography begins with Packard family history and genealogy. Appendix 1 is her understanding of family genealogy. She identifies four lines back to the Mayflower, which as Paul Allen, our oldest son, discovered her lines are incorrect. A little sleuthing shows the problem lies in several people having the same name and second marriages where there were no offspring. There is a line going back to Richard Warren of the Mayflower, but it is not one Georgiana described.

The story then flows into her life in a very religious farming family in the area around Monson and Blanchard, Maine. In an endearing way she talks about common elements of everyday life and in an understated way tells of major life and death events. Besides the labor of clearing farms, taking care of family and helping neighbors, these New Englander's religious convictions caused them to hate slavery.

Georgiana's older sister Hannah, her family, and their older sister Sarah began the Packard immigration in 1855. Georgiana was 11 years old when Cyrus Packard, his wife Sarah, son Samuel and daughters Olive and Georgiana left Maine for Kansas in 1857. They were one family of many New Englanders who moved to Kansas to help insure it would be a Free State. The next part of her story talks about the rugged frontier life as she grew into womanhood. Again in her understated manner, she describes the importance of family, planting crops, drought, disease, and the Civil War.

Her final part of the story includes her marriage to George Washington Packard. When Georgiana was 12, George Washington Packard came to Kansas where he lived with Georgiana's family for a year. George Washington Packard then moved on with his life as a teacher and farmer elsewhere in Eastern Kansas. When the Civil War broke out, he volunteered and spent over 4 years in the Kansas Cavalry. When he returned to Topeka in 1865, Georgiana was a young woman of 20, which I can imagine both shocked and pleased him.

The Bulletin of the Shawnee County Historical Society published in June, 1956, has a number of letters to Hannah, Sarah, and their families from Cyrus Packard, his wife Sarah, and daughters Olive and Georgiana, who were committed to moving to Kansas. The letters describe some of their fears and stoicism regarding their big move to the West.

Another snippet from Georgiana's life comes from the book John Brown by William Elsey Connelley. It tells of John Brown bringing slaves to her father's house as he spirited them north. Cyrus Packard was part of the Underground Railroad. The Appendix includes this information.

We see a little different side of Georgiana in her letters, which are mostly to her mother-in-law Elizabeth Webster Packard. These are more personal, writing about her husband and family and using her mother-in-law as a shoulder to cry on about illness, children, and the difficult frontier life.

The letters of George Washington Packard begin during his student years at Hebron Academy, which was founded by his grandfather, Deacon Barrows. After moving to Kansas his letters reflect the unrest prior to the Civil War, how the home of Cyrus Packard was used as part of the Underground Railroad, and the religious/political convictions of opposing slavery. Occasionally he lets his dry humor come through.

Much of the writing is about more mundane matters of farming, religion, health and the frustration of being so far away from family in Maine. He wrote many of the letters to his mother and brothers while serving with the Kansas Cavalry and talks about Civil War issues from Colorado, Kansas, and Arkansas. His letters talk in a matter of fact manner about John Brown, Jayhawkers, Bushwhackers, and Copperheads; all Civil War terms we learned about in school. These letters provide insight into the Civil War from the perspective of a Private executing the war, which is different from the strategic analysis of politicians and Generals of the period.

In some of the later letters George's grammar and spelling are not as good as when he first left Hebron Academy. It is unknown if he learned frontier language, was not as careful with language, or if some of the earlier letters were cleaned up some by Ruth Allen. In many of the later letters she was careful to preserve the grammar and spelling of George Washington Packard.

By reading the autobiography by Georgiana, her letters, and the letters of George Washington Packard, we get not only a great insight into part of our heritage, but a firsthand discussion of important historical events in our country.

My Common, Remarkable Family

Georgiana's Autobiographical Story

Written sometime after Oct. 26, 1912 and before her death on Feb. 2, 1921

The 17th Century was remarkable in England for the mismanagement of the kingdom and the unrest of the people. Great numbers of the dissatisfied ones gathered what possessions they could and took ship for the New World.

In the year 1638 Samuel Packard with wife and child, from Windham near Hingham, boarded the ship Diligence at Ipswich, and settled in Hingham, Mass. Their children numbered twelve. The third [Zaccheus] married Sarah Howard, and settled in Bridgewater, There were born to them nine children. James [June 2, 1691], son of Zaccheus, married Jemima Keith, and they had five children. The youngest [Reuben] married Annie Perkins. He was one of the celebrated "Minute Men" who went to Lexington and stood with the "embattled farmers" that "fired the shot heard round the world". He joined Washington's army and stayed with it until the close of the Revolutionary War. He settled in Hebron, Me. 1786. He built a mill to grind corn and saw lumber.

Reuben's children numbered 10. His oldest son, Ichabod, who was also in the Revolutionary Army and was Captain of Militia, lived on the old farm. Ichabod married Rachel Cole before leaving Bridgewater. They had seven sons and five daughters, the only one who did not live to old age being Zibeon, who studied for the ministry and died of consumption. Their children were Isaac, Lewis, Ephraim, Zibeon, Reuel, Cyrus, George Washington, Olive, Anne, Hannah, Carolyn and Rachel.

Lewis succeeded to the old homestead. He married Elizabeth Webster, a cousin to Daniel Webster. They had five children - Zibeon, Elizabeth, Hannah, George Washington and Charles. Lewis died when the children were small, but your grandmother was such a capable woman that she kept them together and gave them a good education on the rocky hillside farm. Most of her children were school teachers, and the youngest was a surgeon in the army during the Civil War. Zibeon succeeded to the farm and made a comfortable living with horticulture. His third daughter, Edith, who married Fred Cushman, is occupying the old homestead at present. When your father was young they cut a pine tree and made it into shingles that covered the whole house the tree had been growing more than 2000 years.

John and Anne Barrows sailed in the ship Mary Anne from Yarmouth, England in 1637, settling in Salem, Mass. Their son was Robert, whose son was George, whose son was Peleg, whose son was Joseph, whose son was William, born Jan. 22, 1756. First wife was Sarah Dunham, born July 1756. Their children were Zilpha 1781, George 1783, William, 1784, Patience 1787, Joseph died young, John Stuart 1791, Cornelius 1793. Sarah Barrows died. Wm. Barrows married Catherine Pratt Macumber. Their children were - Caleb, born Dec 22, 1800, Sarah, born June 17, 1803.

Wm. Barrows, born in Carver, Mass. enlisted in the Revolutionary Army when he was a stripling. The story is told of how he, with a number of other soldiers stationed in New York, went in the night to cut down a gilt statue of George 3rd which stood in the street. Barrows stood on the shoulders of two others and tried to sever the head from the body with an axe, but the noise of the decapitation brought the Tories to the scene, who drove the boys away. They finally returned in broad daylight and overturned the statue, finding it was made of lead gilded over. The lead was confiscated by the rebels and made into bullets to fight King George's soldiers.

Barrows served through the war and afterwards settled in the province of Maine, Hebron, Cumberland Co. [Renamed Oxford Co. in 1805]. He helped build a Baptist church there and conducted the services himself when no minister was present. Being greatly interested in the higher education of Youth, he took steps to establish an academy in his chosen town. He rode horse back from Hebron to Boston to place a petition before the legislature asking for a charter and grant of land for the academy. He was granted the charter and the township of Monson Piscataquis Co. Maine given to endow the institution. He built a three story boarding house where the students from abroad were boarded for $1.25 per week, washing included. In 1814 he was elected to the legislature, and while absent his boarding house burned to the ground. Nothing daunted, he burned the brick himself and erected another two story brick building, still standing in good repair and used now as a dormitory. His oldest' son, a graduate of Dartmouth College, was the first principal of the academy. Wm. Barrows, Jr. adopted Wm. Pitt Fessenden when an infant, reared and educated him, and he became M.C. and Secretary of State. The Academy educated many celebrated men, among whom were: John D. Long, Governor of Massachusetts and Secretary of Navy during the Spanish American War; Hannibal Hamlin, Vice President; Judge Bonney; and innumerable judges and preachers.

When the boarding house was burned the town of Paris sent lawyers to argue for the removal of the Academy to that place as being a more thriving town and business center. After they had eloquently argued the case, Deacon Barrows got up, Bible in hand, and read the account of the man with the one ewe lamb, then he sat down and nothing further was said about the removal of his school.

I have heard my Mother tell of how she used to stir up a ½ bushel of meal into brown bread, baking it in large iron basins in a brick oven. I remember seeing the bread trough, as it was called - a huge wooden tray holding perhaps two bushels, which was used at that time.

Deacon Barrows' oldest son, George, kept a locksmith shop where hunters had their guns repaired. His little son, George Whitfield, coming into the shop, took up a gun standing in the corner and snapped when it discharged its contents, killing his father. The boy lived to be an old man but said the accident was "like a black pall over his whole life."

My Mother's mother was a widow when she married my grandfather and she lost one of her children in a very peculiar manner. He was about eight years old when his uncle sent him to a neighbor's to borrow a tool. He was never seen again. It was supposed at the time that he was destroyed by wild beasts, but afterwards that he was accidentally killed by the neighbor.

My father was Cyrus Packard; the son of Ichabod, my mother was Sarah Barrows, daughter of Deacon Wm. Barrows. When they were married in 1825 there was quite an exodus of Hebron young people to the town of Monson. They also founded another town named Blanchard. There were Ephraim Packard whose wife was cousin to Mother, called Sarah Barrows; another of father's brothers, Reuel, whose wife was Mother's cousin Patience Bowker; father's sister, Rachel, who married Jacob Blanchard; another cousin, Atwood Barrows, whose wife was a Webster; Uncle Cornelius Barrows who married Father's sister, Ann; Caleb Barrows, whose wife was Rebekah Beares; another Sarah Barrows, Mother's cousin, who married Thomas Davee, a M.C. Squire; Wm. Bowker whose wife was a granddaughter of Reuben Packard. These with others, always helped each other out in the accidents of pioneer life, also making life more pleasant in their new home.

My father was a remarkable man of good presence, tall, with black curly hair and dark blue eyes. He was very religious. He always had to bear the burdens of pioneer life in a country composed of vast forests and rocky soil, with a climate which had six or seven months of winter, liable to snows six feet on a level. His four oldest boys died in childhood, and the six daughters were not very strong. I think father cleared three farms, cutting off the timber and burning it to get rid of it, building houses and barns, making fences and wells. After every snow he had to get out with oxen and break the roads. It was common for us to have our front windows covered with drifts. Father would tunnel out to the barn to care for the stock. He used to teach school part of the year. My earliest recollections are of life on the last farm which he cleared.

I was born July 11, 1845, youngest of six girls. I was eighteen months old when my parents heard that mother's mother had lost her mind and was put on the town. Father at once got ready a horse and sleigh, and leaving the family in charge of an older sister, he and Mother set out through the snow to go a hundred miles. They arrived home safely with their precious burden. She lived two and a half years after this and was buried in the little mountain graveyard in Blanchard with my four brothers.

Father adopted a homeless infant boy and kept him until he was grown and then he left us. When I was four years old, my brother, Samuel Fessenden, was born and there was great rejoicing among our friends and neighbors. I remember one incident that occurred in the spring before I was four years old. Father and mother were going to Blanchard about three miles distant, to visit Uncle Ephraim, who was Probate Judge for that county. We always walked instead of riding, and they told me I could go. My sister, Olive, wanted me to stay with her, and followed us clear to the big road coaxing me to come back, but I was obdurate. It seems strange that so small a child could walk so far, but we were so used to walking we thought nothing of it. The snow was just going off and the little ditches on either side of the road were full of water, forming all kinds of cataracts and cascades with their musical notes. I remember it as one of the most beautiful walks I ever took, and when we arrived they were all so glad to see us. We had a nice dinner, and afterward my youngest cousin tried to get me to read to her out of the second reader, but I was too bashful and she had to take me to the deserted kitchen to get me to read. When I was three years old my sister Sarah had a long spell of sickness, and I would get a book or paper and go to her, pointing to a word and ask, "What's that?" and, before they thought of it, I knew how to read. I had two books which my sisters had brought to me from Banger, "The Tract Primer" which commenced, "A is for Adam who was the first man", and the other was "Mother Goose's Melodies". I always kept these with me.

When I was five years old the first marriage in my father's family took place. My second sister, Hannah, had always been our main stay. She used to work in the cotton mills in Lowell, Mass. She married a very promising young man named Wm. Jordan. He was a self made man, but if the young men now could know as much as he did, how different they would be. He had a worldwide view and could see everything in the broadest light. He and Hannah were comrades and lovers to the end. They went to live on a farm about two miles away, and when I was six years old Hannah insisted that I come and live with her. She had a special interest in me because I was born the day she was eighteen years old. I always thought at that time that my father and mother did not love me as they did the others, yet I did not think it strange as I was the sixth girl and they needed a boy so not think it strange as I was the sixth girl and they needed a boy so much. I never said anything about it, and I know now it was only a childish mistake. I went to live with William and Hannah Jordan, and I can truly say that they were always extremely kind to me. I used to go home and make long visits and went to school in the village 2 1/2 miles away.

A spirit of unrest was sweeping the Northern states. Wm. Lloyd Garrison, Wendell Philips, Charles Sumner, Joseph R. Giddings and many others were stirring up the people against the hideous crime of slavery. Mrs.

Stowe's "Uncle Tom's Cabin" came out in the National Era which we read every week. Father was one of the first anti-slavery men. His brother Ephraim was much ashamed of him for the stand he took; but when he got Uncle Tom's Cabin, he read it clear to the end with the tears rolling down his cheeks and that minute he became an anti-slavery man. Our people began to get ready to leave their homes with the object of helping in making Kansas a free state.

> "They crossed the prairies as of old
> Their fathers crossed the sea
> To make the West, as they the East
> The homestead of the free".
> > Approximate first and last verses of John Greenleaf Whittier's "The Kansas Immigrants"

Father used to read aloud to me political speeches in Congress and elsewhere, and by the time we children were half grown we were politicians.

William Jordan, his wife and three small boys and sister, Sarah, left Maine for Kansas Nov. 1855. They spent the first winter in Lawrence where they lived in a shack belonging to Gen. Dietzler. They then became impressed with the idea that Topeka would be the capital of Kansas and moved to that place, having bought 160 acres of land two miles south of Tenth Street, which was for years the southern line of the city. There was a log cabin ten feet square on the land, and he put up a tent at one end. Hannah was almost bed ridden for a year with spinal trouble and Sarah had to be nurse and caretaker.

During this time I was with my father's family and enjoyed the year and a half with them with all a child's enthusiasm. The farm where I was born was on a hillside sloping from ledges made of slate, down to a cedar swamp. Father always had to use oxen to plow around the stumps and rocks, and we children picked up the loose stones on the fields and put them in piles to be carted away. There were great boulders on either side of the house as large as a good sized room that we children had for playhouses. To go to school we had to cross a cedar swamp said to be the home of bears. All the fertilizer available was used on the land. A farmer's corn field ran from one-half to three acres, and five acres was a very large field. The Canada Flint corn was the only kind used. We had never heard of sweet corn or popcorn. The farmers raised wheat, oats, barley, rye, peas, and beans, potatoes, and all other vegetables. We always kept cows enough to have some butter to sell, and made cheese enough to last the year round.

Small fruit grew wild. We used to go over the hills searching for strawberries, while red raspberries grew all along by the woods. On high rocky hills grew the red bunchberries, and in the woods the fragrant box berry, which is the wintergreen of commerce. There was a high mountain in Blanchard, called Russell Mountain, and blueberries grew all over it in summer. Father said that, as we were going to a prairie country, we must go up on the mountain before we left, so one morning in August we started with all the baskets and buckets. We rode to the foot of the mountain in a buggy, and leaving the horse there we ascended on foot. Three of Aunt Rachel's girls went with us. It was hard scrambling over ledges and rocks but the blueberries were on the "higher levels" and we kept on. Father said there must have been a thousand persons on the mountain that day. We saw Moosehead Lake, 12 miles away. I counted eleven other lakes from one half to five miles long. We ate our lunch and filled our baskets with blueberries and gladly turned our footsteps toward home. It was harder going down the mountain than up, but we got home all right.

One day Olive and I went to Blanchard and Aunt Patience scolded us for coming without a protector, as Uncle Reuel had encountered a bear on the way from Monson the day before. Bruin was sitting in the middle of the road, and as Uncle Reuel could not go around him he had to get out and threw stones at him to drive him away. Father killed a fat young bear which weighed 100 pounds. They salted down the meat which was very good. The men used to club together when there was a thick crust on the snow in March, and go into the woods on snowshoes, dragging long hand sleds, containing provisions and blankets; when they sighted a moose they could catch it by running on snowshoes for the moose would break through the crust. A moose would supply enough meat for several families, as a full grown one weighs about a thousand pounds. They kept the meat buried in snow. It was very tender and good.

Father used to make shingles and shovel handles to sell. He would bring his workbench into the living room in the winter, as he could not chop enough wood to keep more than one fire going. The summer was more enjoyable than the winter. The Maine woods are now the great summer resort for the people of the east. Lake Hebron lies between Monson and Blanchard, and is a body of clear blue water five miles long.

I will give you an idea of how we went to church in summer. We started early and walked along the shore of the lake two miles. It was a beautiful walk, and sometimes when we would come to the cove, Father would allow us to take off our shoes and wade in the shallow water. Our clothing was not fine enough to be in danger of being spoiled. We had our own pew in the meeting house, and I think the sermon was an hour long.

In those days the ladies did not change their fashions as often as now, and I used to get so tired of seeing the same bonnets year in and year out. Occasionally some enterprising woman would take off the ribbon and set it on differently. I remember old Mr. and Mrs. Tyler. She wore a long green veil over her bonnet. He wore a surtout [a man's frock coat] with collar wide enough to reach to the top of his ears. In prayer time she would stand with face to the wall and veil over her face. He would stand facing the aisle with collar turned up. Excellent, hardworking people they were! Having no child of their own, they adopted two orphans and gave them a good home.

We had Sunday School after preaching. We carried question books with questions and answers on some lessons in the Bible. There was a library, and we got books to read every Sunday, usually memoirs of some remarkable child who died young. At this period of my life I never expected to grow up. After Sunday School we wandered through the graveyard and ate our doughnuts or gingerbread which we carried in our pockets. The monuments and epitaphs were very interesting, and there were many flowers in bloom. I used to have a guilty feeling when I saw the grave of Amelia Hill, because I had found her eating my dinner of brown bread and cheese at school, and had taken it from her. It seemed to me that I ought to have let her have it and that the want of it might have caused her death.

Sometimes my sister would take me into stay a while at Mrs. Whitings', a distant relative. She was a tailoress and employed several women who used to criticize my name, saying how much better they liked Henrietta or Wilhelmina or Josephine, which was a great trial to me, I never like to be singled out for special remarks. At two o'clock we went to meeting again and got out at four, arriving home at five. Mother always had a good hot dinner for us then, and bread and milk before we went to bed.

The days in summer were longer there than here, when a great part of Father's work was mowing and making hay [always by hand] for the stock had to be fed seven months in the year. He used to get up at four o'clock and go to mowing, and mother had breakfast at six and lunch at ten. We children used to help about turning the hay and raking it; Olive used to be a good hand, but I was not strong enough. The black flies were a great nuisance. The winter of 1856 and 1857 we moved to the village and lived in the parsonage, which was empty. Olive and I went to the academy. I remember studying a few weeks with a distant relative who wanted me to help her mornings and evenings. She had no child of her own and, I thought, was rather strict and severe on that account. One morning she bought a nice pair of shoes which she let me wear to church. They were a great deal finer than I had ever possessed and while sitting in church I took shy peeps at them now and then. She told me she had thought of giving them to me but because I had looked at them in meeting she would not. There was a convention of ministers and delegates from abroad: she expected her house to be full. She cooked dozens of mince and pumpkin pies, doughnuts, cake, white and brown bread, and had her meat in the roaster and her potatoes washed. She told me we would go to meeting in the forenoon and she would go home at eleven o'clock to put the meat in the oven, but I must wait until the service was over, then come in and take a certain cloth and go in the parlor and mop up the water from the window sills, which would be running down from the frosty panes. I must not speak to her as she would be too busy to be bothered. All that came to dinner were her brother and his two daughters. I laughed to myself. One day when we had been sitting quietly, she asked me suddenly what Job's wife said to him. She asked me in such a manner I thought I was much to blame for not knowing, but I was forced to acknowledge my ignorance. She told me, and I never forgot what it was, "Curse God, and die."

We were well instructed in the Holy Scriptures, as we always had family prayers in the morning when we all sat down with Bibles in our hands and read the chapters by course, each taking his turn. Then no school was opened without the reading of the Bible and prayer, so that, in a certain sense, the Bible was our "Daily Guide".

In the spring of 1857 we packed our necessary bedding and clothing and came to Kansas. Our company consisted of father, mother, Catherine, Olive, Georgiana and Samuel and a cousin of ours, William Lewis Barrows. Two neighbors took us and our belongings in a wagon on runners to Newport, the nearest railroad station. We spent the first night at the tavern in Dexter, where we had our only experience with New England taverns. The wide rooms were scrupulously clean. The beds were comfortable. We each had both hands full of articles to be used on the way. We carried provisions for the journey and mother had packed a dozen plates, beside knives, forks, spoons and drinking dishes.

It was in the latter part of March that we boarded the train that carried us to Boston, which we reached Saturday night. Sister Charlotte met us at the station. Most of our party went to stay over Sunday with cousins but I went with Charlotte to her boarding house. In the morning we sat down to breakfast at the long tables, and everyone was served with brown bread and baked beans right out of the oven. We spent Sunday with our cousins, the Dunham's, and next day had our picture taken and made some purchases, took the train for Albany, arriving near midnight. We went to a hotel which had been recommended. A young lady, named Sarah Higgins was traveling with us to Chicago, and we four girls were put into a room with two beds in it, which for rags and dirt beat anything I ever saw. We were so tired that we thought we would lie down on the outside of the beds with our clothing on, but one came in and told us this was the wrong room and took us into the next room where there was one decent bed, but others came and told us this was their room and remanded us to the other room. I think we did not sleep much that night and were glad to get out in the morning. The landlord was going to make us pay for our breakfasts although he had been told we carried our own provisions. But a company of Maine men traveling with us got us out of the house in safety.

The next stop of any length was Chicago, where we had to stay a day and a night waiting for our train. We had very good accommodations and here made our introduction to coal fires. There were no sidewalks on the way to the station, and we walked over shoe in mud. We stayed in St. Louis over Sunday. We arrived late in the evening and boarded the ferry to cross the Mississippi River. Mother wanted a drink and father undertook to get it for her. She never dreamed of his leaving the boat for it, but he did, and we left him, of course. Mother was sure he was drowned, but we had the name of King's Hotel, where we were to stop, and the men from Maine, still being with us, led us over miles of streets until we came to King's Hotel where we were shortly joined by father who came on the next boat.

Monday we took the train for Jefferson City, and there boarded a big river steamboat, crowded with passengers, mostly for Kansas, some carrying their slaves with them. This was the pleasantest part of our journey. A long table was set in the cabin, and we were served with wild turkey every day and with very good fare. Our own provisions had run out by this time. The captain and passengers ate at the first table, the crew and waiters at the next, and the colored folks last. My brother and I had never seen any Negroes, and it was a great sight to see so many sitting at the table eating. As we were too polite to stare at them we went into our state room, climbed to the upper berth and looked out of the transom. I think it was a three day's journey to Quindaro, where we stopped and hired a man with a team to take us to Topeka.

The Delaware Indians lived on the land between Kansas City and Lawrence, and we stopped at their houses for dinner and lodgings. The second day we passed through Lawrence, but I did not see much more than an unfinished hotel. We stopped that night at Big Springs where I was impressed with the big whiskers which the men wore, and was perfectly sure our men would not look so barbarous. We rode west on the California road looking for "a house with a brick chimney" about seventeen miles, when we came to it. Father inquired at the door if they could tell us where William Jordan lived. They were so interested they all came to the road to show us the house and to see us. The house was a new log house about two miles away. This man was Samuel Hall from Maine who was one of the earliest settlers of Topeka.

We were soon at the house of our dear brother and sister. The little boys were eating bread and milk out of tin basins, with clam shells for spoons, and they were altogether as wild looking as those of Big Springs; they were so glad to see us that we could not be critical. They had no horses, just a yoke of oxen and a cow. They had to haul all their wood from quite a distance.

Sister Sarah had filed on a claim east of Jordan's and had taken oldest boy, Frank, so she could be the head of a family. They lived on the claim long enough to hold it, but one day when she was cooking outdoors, the fire got away from her and burned out a family of campers, wagon, provisions and all. They came up and sat down by her shack and said she would have to feed them. She fed them the best she could with corn bread and fried bacon, but they soon went away. I think she was disheartened for she got married a few weeks before we arrived and a jumper, named, Lewis, took the claim the day before we came. Sister

Sarah married a widower named Jesse Stone from Massachusetts. His first wife had died from a fall while they were moving in a wagon, leaving him with six children between the ages of two and fifteen, and they certainly needed mothering. They had one bed made of poles in the corner, in the shape of bunks one above another. They built a new frame house that summer where George, the artist, was born. This house was on the Burlingame Road.

William Bowker, son of Squire Bowker, who died in Monson, came to see us, and with him was William Owen from Rhode Island, who had settled in Rochester and was trying to make a town of it. The Town County had induced old Mr. Wendell to file on a quarter section of land, with the promise to deed the south half to them for a town site. They found he was expecting to hold the whole, so they wanted father to go onto it and see if he could not hold it. They built him a cabin and he moved right into it, but Mr. Wendell got there first, so of course won the contest. Then father and mother kept a boarding house in a house owned by Mr. Owen. In the front room father kept a store.

One morning when William Jordan went to Rochester he found mother sitting on a trunk marked George Packard. She was wondering whose it was. About that time Dr. Josiah Jordan came to our house and told us that he had come from Kansas City with George Packard and they had taken turns riding a horse the doctor had bought in Kansas City. Yes, there he was coming over the field, too tired to go around it. We soon had him with his coat off lying on the lounge to rest. He was not such a good walker as father or William Owen, who made nothing of walking from Leavenworth to Topeka. He was just from the academy in Hebron, and tried his hand at jumping a claim where a Missourian was trying to hold two. He got the claim and was elected first acting superintendent of public instruction in Jackson County. At that time Jackson extended to the river. He taught the first school in Rochester.

William Bowker lived with Edward Plummer on claims two miles north of Rochester, and their sisters, Mariah Bowker and Phoebe Plummer, came from Maine in the summer of '57. Some of my pleasantest remembrances are of visits to them in their cabin. How pleasant were those first years, lit with the halo of youth and enthusiasm! The country was raw prairie with nothing on it, but it was free soil, and father was delighted to find a place where he could plow straight ahead without going around stumps or picking up stones.

There were few houses in Topeka, and those were very small. The school house, built by the Emigrant Aid Society, was a brick building 20 ft. Square, whose walls had cracked and were held together with iron rods. We had union services there and Dr. Martin's wife had her melodeon brought over, and Dean Fransworth was superintendent of the Sunday School. Louis Bodwell was one of our first preachers. His two brothers, Edwin and Sherman, were among the first settlers. His father came from Connecticut in 1857 with wife, son Charles and two daughters now Mrs. Perine and Mrs. Staggs of this city.

We always forded the river when it was not high. I have crossed the river when I had to put my feet on the horse's back to keep them out of the water. When the river was high we crossed at the ferry kept by the Kaw Indians. Foot passengers crossed in a skiff for ten cents while wagons crossed in a scow for fifty cents.

The land for two miles north of the river belonged to the Kaw Indians. All the buildings I ever saw on that land were one cabin. Beside it was a grave near which was a pole from which hung a scalp lock. It belonged to an Indian, for it was coarse and shiny.

Father and Mother lived at Rochester, six miles from us. They used to walk to see us frequently. A prairie is a hard place to make a home, as there is nothing there but the land. Everything had to be made by hand or carried a long way. We had no shade trees for many years, which is the reason the old settlers are so unwilling to cut a tree. All the wood we had must be carried a long ways.

The wash pan we used for many years was a knothole cut out of a log. The lack of water was a serious thing. We had to carry water from one fourth to one half mile. Men dug wells as soon as they could but it was sometimes years before they got good ones. Our home life was very plain. We kept cows and chickens, so had our butter, eggs, and meat. Fruit was our greatest lack. Rabbits destroyed all our fruit trees in spite of all the coverings. For twenty years nearly all the fruit we had was brought in wagons from Missouri. We had crabapple, plum, wild grapes, wild gooseberries and strawberries, and if we should have an abundance there was no way to keep it but to dry it. The building was mostly concrete, which was new then and cheaper than frame.

The town had a steady growth, with a country filling up all the time.

We had epidemics of malaria which mostly took the form of fever and ague, but sometimes bilious and typhoid fevers. I have known many times when there were not enough well to care for the sick. The day Albert Jordan was born everyone in the house was sick with a chill but one little boy. Sister Sarah came to help and she had a chill. My chill came on before I got up in the morning and continued until late at night, without intermission. We heard that one of Samuel Hall's daughters, aged ten, had died of a fever. I was the only one who could go there, so took horse and rode two miles, finding them in dire straits. Mrs. Hall was just able to walk by taking hold of things. She had dressed the little girl by wrapping her in a sheet. One of the neighbors, an old bachelor, went to town for the coffin and when he came home with it he had to lay right down on the floor he was so sick. Neighbors buried her, but there was no funeral. The old settlers are like comrades from the army, they have been through so many hard times together. They like to get together and talk them over.

The summer of 1858 Olive taught a subscription school in Mr. Stone's old cabin. I think there were about twenty pupils and she was to board around. There was one family of mullatos [today an offensive term referring to a person with black and white parents], children of black Anne and Chateau; a Frenchman who belonged to the family who owned nearly all of St. Louis. Olive did not wish to board here but thought it would not do to make them angry, so took her turn with them for a week. They had a new frame house which they used for the best room, and they gave her this for her own use. It had a nice bed dressed in white. Mrs. Chateau brought in her meals and stood behind her chair to wait upon her. She fared much better here than with any of us white folks. There was a wooden bridge built across the river in 1858 and Olive walked across the stringers before it was done. The bridge went out in a high water the same summer. Olive was married in 1858 to William Owen.

I joined the Congregational Church when there was no church building in town. There were some business blocks with halls over them which were used for public meetings and subscription schools. There were no public schools for years after we came.

The early settlers had no knowledge of the treasurers of Kansas hidden under the green and smiling surface. The vast beds of coal, salt, gypsum and Zinc; the reservoirs of oil and gas were as unknown to them as to the inhabitants of China. All they thought of was how to raise enough vegetables for themselves and stock.

The year 1860 opened very dry and no rain came in the spring. The crops were planted but did not grow. We looked with longing eyes at the floating clouds, but they did not materialize. The long, hot summer dragged miserably, nothing grew but a little prairie grass. Beans planted in the spring were dug up and grew next spring. The sun's heat was tremendous; one could cook an egg on the stones. The streams were all dried up and the stock was driven to the river for water. It looked as though Kansas was to resolve itself back into the great American desert. In August father took to his bed with typhoid fever. He thought if it would only rain he could get well, but the elements were against us. He died the 3rd of September, aged 63. He was a soldier in the War of 1812; was one of the first temperance and antislavery men, always public spirited and generous. He lies in the Rochester cemetery.

The last days of September were scathing hot. The coffee pot from breakfast was still hot at night, with no fire in the house all day. When I speak of the coffee pot, I do not mean we had coffee; roasted rye ground and sweetened with sorghum molasses served for coffee, and the leaves of red root dried for tea; those were for the elders, we young folks drank water. The poor chickens and dog nearly died of the heat. We were obliged to shut all the doors and windows to keep out the hot winds. Many of the residents packed up and went east. Those who had resources stuck to it, and when winter came the snow piled up and the fierce winds blew. The men had to be on the road all the time hauling supplies from the river towns. Mr. Mosaman, a sturdy farmer from Mission Creek stayed all night one time at our house, on his way to Atchison. His clothes were patched past belief. He said "they put the patches all on him and the others had to go without". His wife used to ravel out muslin and twist it up to make thread. The men wore clothes made of sacks that held relief goods. They said that when those garments were worn to shreds there was still, in bold relief, the letters "S.C. Pomeroy - Beans".

The next year was very prolific and twice as much as usual was raised. W. Jordan got 200 bushels of potatoes off a small piece of ground. He piled them up and fed them to the hogs, as there was no market. We paid a high price for what we bought. Calico was fifty cents a yard. William Jordan bought enough thick cloth to make him and his boys some trousers, paying 95¢ per yard. I made them up and within two weeks there were big round holes in the boys' knees, and then I had to patch them all winter. In 1866 and 1874 there were grasshoppers that ate up every green thing. This gave the state the name of "Bleeding Kansas."

Then came the great struggle between freedom and slavery. The John Brown raid and the hanging of John Brown occurred in the latter part of 1860. Kansas had no part in the first election of Lincoln, for the democratic congress steadily refused to let Kansas become a state, and only by the splitting of the democratic vote was Lincoln elected. Then followed the fall of Fort Sumter and the forming of the Southern Confederacy. Nearly half the men in Kansas sprang to arms. James Lane and others traveled through the state constantly, raising one regiment after another, until it looked as though the whole country was hurrying to the front. When Congress convened in 1881 Kansas was admitted into the Union at once.

G. W. Packard left all his chances for fortune and joined the 9th Kansas, a cavalry regiment, and lived in the saddle most of the time for three years and half his time was spent hunting bushwhackers and escorting trains. Many men left their families and joined the army. I remember Harrison Hannah, an enterprising farmer from Vermont. He left his wife and two little children in Topeka while he hurried away to war. His wife was sick at the time and when she was able to travel was to go to friends in the East. She started with her brother and was taken delirious on the way and died before she reached home. She was one of the first women who gave their lives for the country. Harrison Hannah was one of the founders of Washburn College.

During the last years of the war Daniel D. Bowker, a very eloquent Congregational minister, entered into the service of the then Lincoln College. He travelled in the East lecturing and raising money. He visited Lincoln who gave him a contribution. They erected a large stone building to be used as a school building, and Rev. Bowker hired a nearby house and furnished it for a boarding house. The college was started with a good many pupils in the winter of '65 and '66. Samuel Drake Bowker was the first principal and William B. Bowker the first president of the college.

William Jordan always kept quite a dairy, and the cows could roam at will as there was no herd law. We always made butter and cheese to sell and after a while began to sell milk. The Lawrence raid was in 1863 and we never knew when we might see a gang of free-booters coming to burn our home. More than one hundred and twenty were butchered in cold blood in Lawrence.

The Price Raid was in the latter part of the summer of 1864. The militia of the state was summoned to repel the invaders. Every man between the ages of eighteen and forty-five went to the front. Those between fourteen and eighteen and forty-five and sixty guarded the towns. They had pickets out on every road with carbine and saber.

We had just discovered a harvest of ground cherries in the cornfield and we were so hungry for fruit that we gathered them in great quantities and made preserves with sorghum molasses.

Mrs. W. E. Bowker and I with a horse and buggy which had been left in our keeping, forded the river and went north to Rochester, and on to Edward Plummer's to see how all the women were passing the time. They all seemed full of courage and our men came back all right, but sixteen of the men of Shawnee County were left on the battle field of the Blue. Rev. Mr. Steele died while they were away and there were no men to bury him. Mr. Steele was the first Presbyterian preacher in Topeka. His son-in-law, Charles Whiting, got a furlough that he might bury him.

It was six miles to Rochester from Wm. Jordan's, and we did not often go there, as the ferry cost so much. One morning William and Hannah took all the children and went over, leaving me to keep house. I was fifteen years old. They were out of candles and were going to get some on the way home. There were some tiny pigs to be fed every two hours, beside all the other stock. When night came the cows came up and I milked them, fed the calves and pigs, but no one came and I went to bed in the dark. Next day I had to go to the field to gather corn for the hogs. I cared for everything, and at night was in the dark again. I went out to feed the little pigs and took up one that was cold and dead. This made me feel rather gloomy, but I just knew they would come soon, so I sat down on a bench and waited. All at once a great meteor descended that made as much light as a full moon, and the light kept coming around the corner of the house while I looked in terror to see what it could be. It vanished before I found out what it was so I gave up and went to bed again in the dark. It rained in the night and the cows rubbed down the fence and went away. I had to go to a neighbor to borrow a horse and saddle to go after them. I finally got them home and cared for, the corn brought in from the field, etc. It took hard work until after noon to get the chores done and my clothes were wet nearly to my waist. They arrived that day with the candles. They had not worried much about me. The cause of the delay was this: A man named Hughes, living in Rochester, had raised quite a crib of wheat. He found that someone was stealing it. A man named Ham had filled his sack at the crib and taken it home. The sack had a hole in it that left a trail of wheat all the way. Mr. Hughes took an axe and ran after him. Ham ran into Wm. Owen's house for shelter and Hughes was coming in with the axe. Sister Olive raised an old revolver and pointed it at Hughes, telling him if he came a step further she would shoot him. I think he thought it was time for him to go, so he left. All this stirred up such a hornet's nest that Wm. Jordan was subpoenaed on the jury, and the case was tried then and there, so that was the reason for their staying so long.

I went to school one year in all after coming to Kansas, but I had so much more schooling in Maine that I was better off than my brother who was seven when we came. He was a very hardworking boy who had always wanted a team. When he was 16 years old he earned a team of black horses. My sister Charlotte, with her husband, George Adwers and little son came from Boston in the fall of 1865.

G. W. Packard enlisted in the veteran corps and went to Washington, but, the war was over by the time he got there. He went to Maine on a furlough and visited his mother, sisters and brothers for the last time, arriving home in March, 1866. We were married on the 19th of April following. We lived with mother the first year. My husband and brother went out to plow one morning and the horses were gone, and they never found them. They had to hire horses to do all their work that summer. Our oldest daughter was born at Rochester. That spring 1867, George Adwers bought a dry goods store in Lawrence and my husband went to work in his store. We remained in Lawrence several years.

G. W. Packard was born at Hebron, Me., September 30, 1835. He was the son of Lewis and Elizabeth Webster Packard. His father died when he was eight years old. The boys cultivated the farm and went to school. The girls were always ready to help at anything from teaching school to binding shoes. When George was twenty years old, he went down to Blanchard to work in his Uncle Reuel's factory. He remained there a year and then went home and prepared to come to Kansas, arriving in June, 1857. He boarded with mother for a year or more and then, with Wm. and Maria Bowker, kept house in a small house in Rochester. He took a claim which he afterwards sold for $500.00 and was offered half of land for the money, but refused the offer. This is where North Topeka now stands. He feared the title would not be good as it was Kansas Indian land. In this way most of the early settlers lost their opportunities for wealth. For years after the land was settled the river was the south line of Jackson County but it was decided to add a ten mile strip north of the river to Shawnee.

George Packard, with about a dozen others, bought an ox team and wagon, loaded it with provisions, blankets and mining tools, and walked with it from Leavenworth to Pikes Peak. They found no gold. After this he went to Salina, where he, Henry Barker and others formed a company for making pressed brick. He might have achieved wealth and prominence but gave up all at the call of the government. He served in the army four years and three months, and when mustered out his health was undermined to such an extent that he was never well afterwards. He moved to Butler County in 1870, and went through the old job of building a home on the prairie. We lived in a log cabin for years, where the water and wood had to be carried some distance and our children numbered five when we moved into a house by a big spring. Mother, Brother Samuel and wife, and sister Catherine moved to Butler the same time we did, also Edward Plummer who had married Maria Bowker. Our children walked a mile and three fourths to school, crossing the little Walnut, a treacherous stream, on stones. I have often wondered that they did not drown. Mother died of a bilious fever in 1877. Brother died of congestion of the brain in 1880. Catherine died at our house in 1885. They were all buried in Quito, Butler County. Of our children, Edith and Florence were born at Topeka, Fred at Lawrence, the others on the farm in Butler County. My husband could no longer do farm work, so we moved to Topeka in 1892. We moved to 1934

Harrison Street, April 1, 1893 where we have lived comfortably ever since. My husband died suddenly October 26, 1912, and is buried in Mt. Hope Cemetery. [Topeka].

[Items in brackets and italicized were added by Tony Allen for clarification].

Packard House at 1934 Harrison, Topeka, Kansas

Tony Allen

2 CYRUS PACKARD AND FAMILY LETTERS BEFORE IMMIGRATING

Letters from Cyrus Packard, Sarah Barrows Packard [wife of Cyrus], and daughters Olive and Georgiana published in the Bulletin of The Shawnee County Historical Society, June, 1956, Topeka, Kansas.

Cyrus Packard Gravestone at the Rochester Cemetery near Topeka, KS

BULLETIN
of
The Shawnee County Historical Society

Number Twenty-Five   June, 1956

Published by
THE SHAWNEE COUNTY HISTORICAL SOCIETY
TOPEKA, KANSAS

Shawnee-County-Bulletin-cover.

Cyrus Packard

By Lillian Stone Johnson

This article was prepared by Lillian Stone Johnson, the wife of Judge Beryl R. Johnson and the daughter of Robert Stone, first president of the Shawnee County Historical Society. A descendant of pioneer families she has lived in Topeka most of her life.

In an article in the Topeka State Journal of June 2, 1954 written by Gordon P. Martin, he says. "There is one burial that particularly attests to Rochester's [cemetery] venerability. The name of the deceased was Cyrus Packard. And he was a veteran of the war of 1812."

I know about him through my Grandmother Sarah Packard Stone. He was her father. Grandmother Sarah had come to Kansas in 1854 with her sister Hannah and Hannah's husband, William Jordan and their three little boys. The father Cyrus and his wife, Sarah Barrows Packard, stayed in Monson, Maine with the two smaller children, Olive and Georgiana. The following letters were written to my Grandmother Sarah, her sister, Hannah and Hannah's husband. The Jordan family was at that time on the quarter section on the corner of which is now Avondale School. Aunt Hannah named the farm, "Avondale." The little boy referred to is Josiah Jordan. who became County Superintendent. Olive and Georgiana, respectively fourteen and ten years old at the time of writing became the wives of William Owen and George Packard [Georgiana's cousin] and reared large families here in Topeka. Cyrus Packard at this time was 60 years of age.

Monson, Maine—1856

Dear Sarah and Hannah:

Ever since that memorable morning you bade us goodbye. Mother has been selecting things to carry with us and everything designed to move is taken care of, even some things you left behind. Our movements are tardy but people begin to think that we shall go if a good providence opens the door.

I have been laid up a long time this winter with a cough and cold but for some time my health has been good. I do wish you would answer some questions as well as you can. First could an able man live there without money or is there any call for labor and what compensation can a man get for his work? Second, were there any good crops raised there last year and what kind of crops did the best? Third. what are the prospects of the coming season, was there much wheat sown? Is there much ground plowed? Are teams ready to keep the plows awake in the spring? Fourth, is there any timber there that will make good shingles? Are boards seasoned and can you procure good stone in your locality - and what are they used for? Can they make brick most anywhere in your section? Have they got good milk in Topeka? Many questions like these. I know enough about a new country to know that many such questions can't be answered definitely.

Many say here that they would like to go to Kansas were it not for the climate many say they would like to go on that account. I am fully of the opinion that whoever goes there will acknowledge a great change and it is right that we should carry our customs there with us as far as it is for the best. Those that are first on the ground will do much to mould future society and how important it is that a right influence should take precedence at first.

War is a desolating evil to morals as well as to life and oh what an awful curse rests on the authors of our political calamities. Were Benedict Arnold alive he would have friends enough in Washington and elsewhere.

We have to announce the death of Solomon T. Dana. He died in Ohio. His leg got well and immediately he was seized at the lung with a bad cough. The doctor told him he had better go south. About two months ago he went to Ohio to the Buttons. Yesterday we read intelligence of his death. He will be buried in Monson. The widow will probably accompany the remains to this place.

It is no use dear children to tell you how much we miss you. We have been very much secluded of late, but it is a comfort to talk to you on paper, yes a comfort the thought that your eyes will run over this scribbling. May the Lord bless you all.

Cyrus Packard

Monson, February 23, 1856, Morning

Dear Brother and Sisters:

I have set myself to write you a few lines though I do not know as I can write anything that will interest you. It is pleasant morning this morning. It has blowed and blowed. Our door is all covered over with snow, so that we have to go through the shed. We have some of the greatest drifts anywhere around. School finished Thursday. We have had one of the pleasantest schools I ever attended. I have not told you what I studied this term. I studied arithmetic history and philosophy. I have bought me a History and a Course of Time. I have got half through philosophy. Hattie Bailey, Henry Stinchfield, and Henry Haines and I were all that studied it. I have had my hair cut off two to three months and it curls as well as Charlotte's all over my head. So you see that my wish is gratified now.

Georgiana and I went to Mr. Pool's yesterday. Helen has had a cough all winter. Ann wants to know if they need tailors out there. I have had my plain delain dress washed and turned wrong side out and upside down. I have bought me a calico for me a full waiste and apron. I have my woolen dress on. Mother says she wishes you had some like it. Mother is boiling beans today for dinner. Georgiana scolds about my collars. She feeds her lamb and I my colt.

She is one of the most gentle horses I ever saw. You must not think this is a sample of my writing for my pen is poor.

Dear Frankie, How I would like to see you very much indeed. Grandma thinks that your top and sled are too heavy to carry but I guess that we shall bring your mineoteu [?] and book.

Dear Carol, I am sorry that you have so many bumps on your head and that you have had your curls cut off. I don't believe that you will ever look so pretty again as you did when you went away. I'd like to kiss you.

Dear Josiah though I think that you have got a rather homely name, I guess that you are a pretty boy and am glad that you have got so good a mother.

Olive A. Packard

p.s. I should like to know what kind of a school it will be for me to keep out there, if I get qualified. Sarah, I think that you had better look out about going over there. You may have to live in that log hut.

[Jesse Stone had lost his wife and Sarah Packard had gone over to look after him and his six children. Jesse Stone's farm was where the Foster Cemetery is now and his first wife's grave was the first grave on that ground. Sarah married Jesse Stone the following January 8, 18S7. They were the parents of George Melville and Robert Stone.]*

   * Editor's explanation.

Monson 1856

Dear Frank and Carol and Little Josiah:

I guess your mother and father laughed some at your letters before they sent them. Mother laughed so she could hardly read them. I hope I shall be able to come to Kansas next fall if not next spring. If the naughty folks act so bad that we cannot go out there we want you to come back here. Olive and I have been sliding this morning and wished that you were here to slide with us. I am knitting a pair of stockings for Kansas.

Affectionately,

    Georgiana Packard

[The following letter is to Sarah and Hannah from their mother Sarah Barrows Packard]

Dear Children:

I wish you had taken another blanket. I have saved cloth for a skirt I will do the best I can for you. Mr. Emerson has been here and made us a very pleasant visit. He is just such a man as you would like and seems to fill the place where Mr. Isley was deficient. Mr. Isley says he is so homesick he could sit down and cry heartily.

I have got out my web for Mrs. Giggins. I shall have about nine shillings for weaving it. Father has had an offer of fifty dollars for his horse and thirty-five for his cow. Had it come in season I think we would have been there before this time. Charlotte [married daughter who lived in Boston] is coming home to make us a good visit. She sent money to pay for Olive's tuition, the preceptor spoke highly of Olive's scholarship. He says she ought to have an education.

I was called out this morning about three o'clock to go down to Mr. Thomas'. Their babe was dying--I laid it out. It was nothing but skin and bones. It could not nurse. It suffered everything. How are my little grandchildren? I hope they are well. I can't get to see them if they are sick or any of the rest of you. I cannot minister to any of your wants.

Last Sabbath night there were about two hundred at meeting. Amory Tyler was there. Father went over to Mr. Gordon's yesterday in hopes to get the mail we failed of getting but we have been so often disappointed we have not much hope there is any letter from you. How hard it is to be so far apart. We fear there is trouble in the mail. We have heard there is something of the kind. Father has gone to meeting tonight. It was quite cold and squally this morning. Father has got in some wheat.

Old Albion Jackson's wife is to be buried today. She died very suddenly-- bled in the lungs-- was about the house the day before she died.

We don't hear very much to encourage us about having peace in Kansas. We have many Fears. Father has gotten home from meeting --says that Mrs. Bowker has had a letter--said nothing about you. Our cows do well--butter is twenty cents a pound. Father got a barrel of flour and a bushel of corn not long since with shingles.

I have been washing today and am very tired. I wish I could see you all but how uncertain are all our creature comforts. I never did think my children would go so far from me but there is rest for the children of God. O that we all may be worthy to enter that rest where there will be no more separation.

Dear Frank I have no little children here to call me Grandma--none that I love as I do you and your little brothers. I want you to be a very good boy and mind your mother. Hannah you said nothing about your lameness in your back. I hope it is better. I have been quilting on another quilt. Fixing some things for a carpet. I have little hope that they will reach Kansas in the present state of affairs but I hope for the best.

We do not expect that you can hold on to that claim Sarah, but it may be that we shall live on it yet who knows--Aunt Sally has just got back from Hebron. She says Uncle Caleb's folks are well--the girls are both at home. Our school begins next Monday. Mr. Emerson's ordination takes place tomorrow. I hope you will write often-- I want a line if no more.

From your Mother

Tony Allen

May 25, 1856

Dear Children:

I wish you would write Mr. I. Phillips as he thinks of going out there if he meets with suitable encouragement – a line from you giving a general view – there is perhaps no one who manifests a greater interest. I think he will go out next fall and Mr. Gates too if he can sell his place. In regard to ourselves we are not too anxious but we cannot feel willing to submit to the thought that we shall see you no more.

I suppose Sarah has been jumped or relinquished her claim and that there is no chance for me near you – do let us know about it. I understand there will be sales in June. In what part of the territory I have not learned which gives me warning of the invalidity of presumptions unless the necessary funds are at our disposal. Sarah, I want you to stay in with William for 1/4 of the land warrant on some terms, so that if we go there we shall not be driven from our homes by ruthless speculators. It seems to me so important that I should fear to go there without some such arrangements.

... our best men confined as traitors or fleeing from ruffian power -- but there is One who is able to deflect the machinations of wicked, designing men and while we would defend every man north and south in their rights, we would claim and demand the same protection from them. Surely the wickedness of our President has caused the people to mourn.

In my last I made you acquainted with the reasons why I am not with you, your political troubles would not deter me from coming and would that I could carry our good Maine men with me for there are thousands here who would be glad to go could they change their property into money. Be of good cheer, God reigns, he regards his own people in mercy and will certainly heed their cry, pray always. Do write and let us know how you get along. Am at your service tho comparatively feeble. Am ready to go as a farmer or a soldier.

Your Father,

Cyrus Packard

Dear Sisters:

I have a little place left to fill. My pen IS very poor. Georgiana and I have just returned from Blanchard. Went over last Tuesday and expected to return Saturday but were detained because of rain. When I hear bad stories about Kansas it seems as tho there will certainly be war there. But God reigns and I trust all to him and let him do what seemeth good in his sight. I have got me a Florence bonnet trimmed in white, the bare bonnet cost $1.25.

Olive

Dear sisters and brother:

I don't know as I can write anything that will interest you but will try to do as well as I can. I go to school and try to learn. I study Arithmetic, History, Geography and Tours Grammar and writing. I like the teacher well. It is so dark I can't see to write.

    Georgiana

Tony Allen

July 6, 1856

Dear sisters and brother:

It is bath morning. I guess we shall go to meeting today. It was pleasant day before yesterday, the fourth of July. We went down to Mr. Thomas' bower in the woods. Olive and I carried some tarts and cheese. We had a nice time.

Father sheered my sheep the other day and got wool enough for me two pairs of stockings. I don't feel like writing this morning at all. I do not think much about Kansas. I don't believe I shall ever take so much comfort there as I do here, but if I thought I should never see you again I would go.

From your sister,

Georgiana Packard

[Following the letters in the Bulletin are excerpts from Georgiana's story, which is presented in its entirety in Chapter 1 so will not be duplicated here.]

3 GEORGIANA PACKARD LETTERS

Letters from Georgiana Packard after her marriage to George Washington Packard mostly to her Mother-In-Law Elizabeth Webster Packard who still lived in Hebron, Maine. Georgiana on the left and Elizabeth Webster Packard on the right.

Tony Allen

[Letter from Georgiana Packard to her new Mother-in-Law, Elizabeth (Webster) Packard]

Topeka, Kansas

April 28, 1866

My dear Mother,

If I may call you by that holy name. I suppose you should like to hear from your youngest daughter. We have neglected writing longer than we should for the want of time and opportunity. I have taken George under my special care and shall try to do all that a faithful, loving wife can do to promote his happiness. I think I realize something of the solemn obligations I have taken upon myself and look only to God for strength to fulfill them. I am perfectly satisfied with my choice, (as indeed I could not be otherwise) and look forward to a life of happy usefulness. We are living with Mother this summer and George is at work with Samuel farming. He says he never enjoyed work so well in his life as he does now. It was rather hard after his four years' service to go right into hard work and his hands that were softer than mine have been used very hard. I think I have never seen you although I remember the time when you and Elizabeth came to Blanchard on a visit. If I had had any idea then of the relationship we should assume in after years, I should have taken a great deal of pains to have seen you. I am very glad that you are acquainted with my mother and sisters and should rejoice most sincerely if I could visit you and get acquainted with my relatives and friends there. I am very sorry that George cannot be with you more as it is one of the greatest blessings to be near one's own family. I hope circumstances will be such that he will not be kept away from you so long again.

I sent the Independent to you not knowing that you took it as I was getting up a club for the premium. I am sorry you have to pay postage for nothing but perhaps you can let someone else have it.

My sewing machine came a week ago and we set it up without any trouble and it works beautifully. Thank you for your present. I will keep it to remember you by. I am very sorry that you have such a trial with Hannah. I should be glad to help you if I could. Mother has had a very hard time taking care of Catherine through her life, but it is no comparison to what you go through every day.

May the Lord help you as He will surely reward you for your self-denial.

From your loving daughter

Georgiana Packard

[Letter from Georgiana to her Mother-in-Law, year unknown] Dec. 2nd

Dear Mother,

As George commenced a letter to you a week ago, I will try to finish it. We were very glad to receive your last as indeed we always are, and to hear that you were well. I have been sick so long that I hardly know how it seems to be well. Mother went to Lawrence and stayed three weeks and while she was gone, I was quite smart, but I suppose I did too much as we had strangers here, and took a severe cold, so that I have been laid up for the past week. Happily, Mother came home Monday, so that we have got along. George has been pretty well, only his hands trouble him a great deal. He has been chopping wood for a day or two which is very bad for them.

The revival is still going on here. A good many, some of them hard cases, are coming out on the right side. We have an Evangelist preaching here who seems to be a remarkable man. He is much interested in laboring for these people as though he had known them for years. He already knows the names and history of the people in this neighborhood better than we do. I think there will be quite an accession to the church here. Ten or fifteen, perhaps more will unite with the Cong. that numbered only four or five before. Among them will be Olive and Samuel. They are the last ones of the family to join the church, and Mother will see one great desire of her life accomplished if they become faithful Christians. I hope this work will affect a great good here. I was quite sick.

George said he wished we could spend the day in Hebron. It seems a long ways in the distant future to think of going back there, but perhaps it is nearer than I imagine. We had a letter from Ella a week ago. She wrote as though she had a new attraction in Hebron but did not tell us what it was so the rest of you must inform us. I am glad to hear that she has such a nice organ. Perhaps we shall hear her play on it sometime. We have had no hard storms here yet. Once in a while a little rain. The fall has been very mild. Mr Plummer's folks from Waterford will move out here in the winter. I do not know whether they will settle here or go further west. They will take a farm and go to raising stock. We have had no letter from Charles for a long time. I think he should write oftener as he has no family cares to occupy his attention. I believe we wrote last to Zibeon and Ellen. Give my love to them all and tell the dear little girls that they have got an aunt away out in Kansas that loves them and wants to see them. Give my love to all inquiring friends and keep a good share for yourself, from you.

Loving daughter, Georgiana

Tony Allen

[Letter from Georgiana to her Mother-in-law.]

Eldorado, Kans.

July 2, 1870

Dear Mother,

We were much pleased to receive a letter from you some time ago. I think if you can find time and strength to write such good letters, that we certainly ought to answer them. The children bother me so much that it is almost impossible for me to write. We have been well so far, only Florence has had some little sick spells. Edith says, "Tell Grandmarm I want to see her deffully" Her sight continues about the same that it was in the spring. We have little hope of her eyes getting better only by an operation. Her general health has been a great deal better the past year than it ever was before. Florence is the most mischievous baby that I ever saw. She is a great deal of relation to the boy who used to throw wheat into the well.

We had an accession to our company of immigrants. Mother came "down south" with Mr. Plummer's wife and baby. Mother went home with Samuel about three miles from here so that I have not seen her yet. She was very tired and I am afraid will be sick. Mr. Plummer's folks live only a few rods from us. They have a little girl seven months old. She looks very much like the Crafts. George has been at work very hard all the time only when it is too hot. We have had uncommonly hot weather this summer. G. thinks when he gets rich he will move back to Maine. He has a great deal to discourage him. His sod crop does not look promising but I hope we shall get something. We have some nice pigs growing and quite a number of young cattle. I think few families can live on a smaller amount than we can. We have been without vegetables so long that we have almost forgotten that we ever had them.

George's greatest trouble is about paying for his place. If he could have had the money to pay for it last April he could have bought half of it on account of it's being in the shape of an L. We had a terrible storm two weeks ago which blew down over forty houses in Eldorado and destroyed a great deal of property. We expected our house to go over although it is locked at the corners and built of large logs. We had a stream of mud and water poured over nearly everything in the house although rain hardly ever comes into our house. George has begun breaking of five acres for winter wheat. We are all so absorbed in trying to get started in life that there is danger of our forgetting a great deal of good, encourage our Faith and strengthen our feeble minds that we may try to emulate her example. If I thought we could bring up our children as we were brought, I should be so glad. We have no churches and no society here yet, but I hope such things will come in time. There is a shower coming up and I must go and get things ready for it. Will try to write a little more bye and bye. Love to the children and all inquiring friends and a great deal to yourself from your loving daughter.

Georgiana Packard

Mother, you must overlook our short comings in writing for it is next to impossible for either of us to write a word. We are prospering nicely now and shall come out all right.

[Letter from Georgiana to her Mother-in-Law]

Lawrence, Kans

May 11, 1872

Dear Mother and friends,

We are to blame for neglecting writing so long, but we are always waiting for a more convenient season. We had a letter from Zibeon two or three months ago. We want to hear from you very much. We had a little boy born the 25th of March. He is very small, but is growing nicely. He looks very much like Edity. We think of calling him Frederick. The girls are having better health than they did have. Edith had the ague hang onto her all winter. We are hoping that her eyes are getting better. The white spot in her eyes is growing smaller and I think she can see some better. The doctor has just been here and vaccinated the children.

I have been in hopes that Mother would make us a visit soon. Sarah went down there on a visit some time ago and was going to bring Mother home with her. Her husband has three children living down that way with their families. I haven't seen any of our folks at Topeka since we came here.

There have been the most wonderful revivals here and in other parts of Kansas that I have ever heard of. I think there have been something like a thousand conversions here, a great many of them very hard cases. I haven't been able to go to any of the meetings and don't know when the time will ever come that I can get out again. But if we can only be bringing up our children as well as we were brought up I shall be satisfied. But I sometimes despair of that.

Try to write a few lines to let us know how you are.

From your affectionate daughter and sister,

    Georgiana

[Letter from Georgiana to her Mother-in-Law]

Quito,

May 27, 1877

Dear Mother

We haven't heard from you since March and would like to know how your health is this spring. We have been having two weeks of very wet weather so as to retard putting in the crops. The grasshoppers did not hatch out this spring here. George has rented out twenty acres of ground to put in corn. He will get half the crop in the field. He will have nearly two acres of potatoes and half an acre of sorghum besides garden vegetables. He planted a bushel of Osage Orange seen on shares this year. He will have half the plants next spring. We have all been to meeting today. We go at nine in the morning to Sabbath School and the Methodist preacher preaches afterwards. The children want me to tell you that they all got some very pretty [chromos] at S. School today. The baby behaves very well in meeting. Samuel's folks were there and Josiah Jordan. He is keeping school six or eight miles from here. He is called one of the best teachers about here, gets from 30 to 35 dollars a month. Sister Emma is keeping school at 32 dollars a month. She makes between 40 and 50 lbs. of butter a week, nights and mornings. She makes the best butter of anybody about here. Mother has not been quite so well lately. I am afraid she has too much work to do.

We think you have a very nice looking family of girls there. They must get a good education and come west as teachers. Teachers make the most money of anybody in this county now.

Edith wants me to tell you that she is trying to get a prize that is offered in S. School. The Superintendent offers a pocket Bible to scholar who repeats the most verses from the Bible.

George went to Mr. Plummer's to a log rolling last night. They put up the logs to make a stable by moonlight. The farmers are all so busy now that he could not get anybody in the day time. Frank Jordan's folks have a nice little boy about two months old.

The children have bothered me so much that I could not write a good letter.

Edith wanted to write a letter to her cousin. I doubt if she will be able to read it. I hope you will encourage the children to write for it is so much easier for them than for older people. We all send our love to you and all the rest of family.

Truly yours,

Georgiana Packard

[letter printed on back of Georgiana's letter from Edith to her cousin Edith]

Dear Edith,

I got your letter and picture. I thank you very much. We never have any maple sugar or apples. I have got a calf and eight pigs.

From Edith

*This letter in handwritten form is shown in the appendix.

[Letter from Georgiana Packard – recipients unknown, could not be her Mother-in-Law since she died on March 26, 1879.]

July 30, 1888?

Must be 1888 as 62 yr old Sarah was born 2/1/1826

Dear Friends,

I will add a few words to Geo. Letter. The past week has been a terrible week. Every day seemed hotter than the last. The thermometer ranges from 100 to 110 and the crops are all killed with the heat and the sun. Potatoes are cooked in the ground. G. has to drive the cattle to the Little Walnut to get water. He dug a well yesterday in the bed of the creek and got enough water for us to use for which we are very thankful.

My health is so poor that I can do no hard work. I have to keep very quiet, have chronic Bright's Disease and the Dr. gives me no hope that I will ever be strong again. If our children could only have their eyes cured we should not worry so much about leaving them.

Sister Sarah and her husband were here on a visit last May. She is sixty-two and he is over eighty. He is a smart man for his age. His hair is not so white as George's, but he is breaking down. Their oldest son, George, is in Paris studying art. The other one is bookkeeper in a big Mill forty miles south of here.

The children want to know Mabel's address so that they can write and get her to send her photograph. Thank you for the paper you sent. I have hard work to get enough reading to occupy my mind. Florence and Fred have to be our standbys. I don't know what we would do without them. Florence has to give up going to school any more. She is giving music lessons now to a young lady friend, will get five dollars for the first 24 lessons. She has a great talent for music.

Give my love to all the family and write soon. Tell us how Ella is situated.

From yours truly,

Georgiana Packard

4 GEORGE WASHINGTON PACKARD LETTERS

Young George Washington Packard on the left probably taken in Hebron, Maine, and older George Washington Packard on the right following the Civil War, probably in Topeka, Kansas

Hebron, [Maine],

Jan. 15, 1854

Dear Brother Zibeon,

I write you a few lines this eve to let you know how we are prospering at home.

My health is good and also the rest of the folks. Our school has kept now 5 weeks and will keep 3 more, and we have a middling good school notwithstanding their trying to shut up the school house.

The colt is doing tip top this winter, and I hope you will find him worth $50 or more next spring than he was when you left home. I have hired Ezra's sleigh for $2 this winter. The cattle are doing well and I think that we shall have some hay left. We cut some wood, before the school, in the woods and we shall have a tier of wood left in the shed after the school is done.

Now you wrote in your last letter that you had become acquainted with a "young lady" that you speak of as being one of the finest of ladies, and that you have spent three evenings with her, courting we suppose. Curious enough! Strange! Wonderful! Funny! Mysterious! and unexpected! Although natural! "Why" now if she is handsome I should like to have you bring her down the next summer as you intended to. I will have thing to satisfaction if you intend to have her. We expect you will create quite a sensation when you bring home your dowsabel.

I have been hoping that I could go to school next fall to the academy in order to teach next winter, but if you wish to remain there another year, we shall try to plant what we can and carry on the farm as well as we can hoping that when you return you will be as "rich as mud."

Mother says she hopes you won't marry for property. Mr. Blake sends his respects to you etc. etc.

I suppose that you're looking for something as it regards politics in

Maine legislature next. Last week there was not a quorum in the senate but a majority were "rumies" and they could not do anything till they went into convention with the house and chose men to fill the vacancies. The house being a majority temperance men we expect that they will elect the remainder of the senators good Maine law men.

We shall send you the first important news that we get in the papers. I had a letter from Horace a short time ago. I have got out of thought so I must close in hopes that you will excuse all mistakes.

Give my respects to Uncle Washington and folks.

Yours without doubt,

George Washington Packard

Will you write that lady's name? Give my respects to her. Please write as soon as convenient. My pen is poor and hand unsteady and head empty.

Kanapolis,

Oct.27, 1857

Dear Brother,

I received a letter from you the other day and was glad to hear from you and glad to know that there was one that had not forgotten me, for I had not heard a word from anyone for a lot of weeks. I am glad to know that you are enjoying good health, that you still go to school, and still enjoy the blessings of a home.

Well, if you could be out here and have the fever and ague for two or three months I reckon you would want to see Marm every day. I wish I could see one more well day such as I used to have at home. I expect to spend all of my money before I can go to work again. I am able to be out of doors a part of the time, instead of being able to make money. I shall not come out as well off as I was by more than one hundred dollars.

I can hardly express my feeling on hearing of the death of Grandmarm that I should never see her again. Still I could hardly expect to see her again when I left for she had passed the common age of many, but perhaps she is but one of the large number of my friends in the east that I never shall see again.

I was sorry to hear that Maine had lost one of her best statesmen for it is a loss to me, all New England and country. I mean Wm. Lesenden.

The Kansas election resulted in a large majority Free State although there were some large frauds on the ballot. We are bound to have Kansas a free state and there is no getting around it.

I expect some of the letters and all of the papers [for I have not received one yet] are stopped on the way. So I hope you will write often for I am not going to write [before] getting an answer, but I think there is more that way that I want to hear than there is here that you want to hear.

We had three nigger runaways stop at our house as a depot for the underground railroad for Canada. They left Topeka two hours before thirty (some) United States troops arrived there. They were conducted here by a minister of the gospel with a revolver at his side. They go up the Lane Trail road through Nebraska and Iowa and so on. The United States troops are worthless things here [the writing in this part of the letter gets very blotched Ruth Allen]. Plague take the paper or the pen I don't know which. My love to all the family and to the folks.

Yours sincerely,

Geo. W. Packard

Salina

Sept. 22, 1860

Dear Mother,

I have just returned from a prayer meeting conducted by Wm. A. Phillips the chief proprietor of the town and a very prominent man in the politics of the territory and correspondent of the New York Tribune here during the troubles in Kansas. He is a very interesting and worthy man.

As another of my birthdays has rolled around it is natural that I should look back upon my past life and think how varied and checkered has been my life. But I think it has not been thrown away altho I wish I had made better improvement of my time than I have. But may I strive to do better in the future.

No doubt you have heard of the death of Uncle Cyrus ere this. I will enclose a letter that I received from Wm. E. Bowker a short time after he died, which is all the particulars I have of his death. I think he left his family in a better condition than he would have done had he stayed in Maine. He was a good old man and I respected him for his integrity and moral worth. And Aunt Sarah has been added to the list of widows in the Packard family.

You probably too have heard of the almost famine in Kansas. There has been scarcely anything raised in the territory this year and that on top of the extreme hard times that the people of Kansas have suffered, it is awful in the extreme, thousands are leaving the territory, some for the winter and some to stay. The Smokey Hill country will not feel it so bad as the more eastern part of the territory for most of the inhabitants hunt buffalo and get their own meat and send a great [part?] to market besides the hides and tallow all of which bring a good price.

I have no family to take care of and have no fears about living through the winter.

Tony Allen

What kind of crops have Zibeon raised this summer and how are the times in the east? I have not heard from home for some time. I expect I have letters in Topeka but have no chance of getting them. I hope, however, to get them soon if there are any there.

Address to Topeka as usual. My love to you all. Write often, if I don't get your letters, presume I shall get some of them. My love to you all.

Yours from your son,

George

My Common, Remarkable Family

Salina, Kansas

June 9th, 1861

Dear Sister Hannah,

As week after week rolls on without any letters from home, I am getting quite anxious to hear. I received a letter from Zibeon a short time after he was married, and answered it at once. I have since then written one to Chas, and to Elizabeth and now I am trying to write to you. I have got none from any of you since the one that Zibeon's wife wrote a week after they were married.

I should like to know how you think you would feel out here in an almost wild country without a solitary relative in a hundred miles of you, probably you think it would be fun. I have friends, of course, and if I found I had not I should leave, but by the time you have been over the world as much as I have you will find that there are no friends like a mother or brothers or sisters. I don't know but a wife should come in the same rank, hope so at least, for I mean to get one as soon as I get old enough. I suppose Zibeon wishes that he had been married ten years ago now, don't he? I think that if the New England Relief committee would send two or three thousand girls to Kansas this fall there would be as great a demand for them as there was for the provisions they sent last winter, and a much happier state of things would be here about them than there was about the relief goods.

I am very anxious to hear from home. I have written as many letters since I have been here as you all. You will direct your letters after this to "Salina Kansas" and I shall get them. Can't you send me a paper now and then? I don't care what it is, anything from home.

Send me an envelope [if] you don't want to write or don't want to send a paper. I write this to you all and if you all get a little mad, just enough to write, I don't care how saucy a letter you write, let it come. Don't send them to Rochester nor anywhere else til I get one.

Tony Allen

I have a fine garden, have picked one mess of peas, there is a lot more on the vines now. I wish you would come in tomorrow and cook them for me. Won't you? Have had radishes a long time, have tomatoes and cucumbers and potatoes in bloom, onions most big enough to eat.

My love to you all until I hear from you,

Yours truly,

George W. Packard

Salina, Kansas

July 14, 1861

My Dear Mother,

In these times of trouble when all true men hold themselves ready to fight for their country, I think it behooves us to write as often as we can, for while we feel an anxiety for our country, we still feel the same anxiety for our friends.

I trust that your intelligence, patriotism and Christianity give you strength to stand under all the trials that you are called on to pass. I am glad that I have friends that are engaged in the defense of their country, although I am very sorry that there is any cause for it.

The Indians are all quiet and manifest a disposition to behave themselves during the war. I wish I could say the same for the Missourians and cannot. C. Jackson, the Governor is in South Kansas with an army but it is rumored that he is in a position that he can't get back to Mo. for Kansas boys are hard to whip and Jackson has got to break the lines of the Kansas boys before he can get back. I hope he will be caught, army and all.

We are talking some of taking part of our company below, that is those that can well leave, men without families like myself. We are of no earthly use to the country as we are and why not go. I don't believe in being idle, neither do I believe in being rash, but if duty calls, I go.

You shall hear from me often whenever I can. Please write on the reception of this and direct to Salina, Salina Co., Kansas

Yours truly

From your son,

George W. Packard

Tony Allen

Osawatomie, Ks

Feb 25, 1862

Dear Brother,

I received the other day, a letter from you and Mother and at the same time one from Wm. and Elizabeth all which were a great treat. I have had no time since I got them to write in consequence of being on the move most of the time. But we are again in camp on the Osage river and in the same town that John Brown's fame commenced where the world first heard of him. It is a fine town altho all of the most of the time, portions of the inhabitants have left for parts not so much exposed to the Rebel Army.

My health is good and am getting along well although inactivity has made me awfully lazy. I hope the service will not spoil me for life.

I think the prospects are good for a speedy termination of the war, altho at an expense of blood and tears. There is but little prospect of our regiment getting disbanded and but little show of our getting into a fight. You need not fear for my safety for I don't believe I shall ever get a chance at the rebels. I have not heard from Charles for several days. Hope to get a letter from him soon. Oh how I long to have this rebellion crushed out. How I long to hear that the last gun has been fired and the last saber returned to its scabbard. When the bugle and fife and drum shall cease to call to arms the thousands of volunteers that are now engaged in the defense of their country and their country's honor, still I cannot say that I want peace until the last slave is liberated and the stars and stripes shall float over a land where all can look to it for protection.

I shall try to write to Wm. and Elizabeth in a day or two. Please give them my love, also to Mother, Hannah and yourself Yours with much respect, From your brother,

George W. Packard

Troy, Kansas,

April 22, 1862,

Dear Brother Zibeon,

It has been a long time since I have heard from home or from Charles and as I have been most of the time on the march for a month or two, I have had no chance to write. However you will be all the [gladder] to hear from me now. We don't get much fighting here to do, so we have to march around from one place to another to quell riots, enforce law, and catch jayhawkers, while at heart we are all jayhawkers.

Our company was transferred from the 8th to the 2nd, and then from the 2nd to the 9th in which we now find ourselves today as at "A".

I have good health all the time; no bullets have bothered me yet. Hard bread and old bacon are the worst enemies I have had to contend with.

I am very anxious to hear from Charles as it is probable that he has had a chance to try his courage since I heard from him. The war has been more terrible than anyone could have looked for. It is depopulating the country fast, and though we are making glorious victories, still we cannot rejoice over it as we would knowing that so many of our friends are constantly being killed or wounded. I think that 3 or 4 months will put a stop to the rebellion in a measure so that the army can be reduced to a smaller force.

I have not been out of the service but three days since I joined. I wish I was out for I think that the West has no use for so many soldiers. Three or four regiments are about to cross the plains for New Mexico. The poor fellows don't like it and are deserting every day. It would be a hard trip but I should like it first rate for adventure don't bother me at all and the more danger the more it suits me.

I don't know why it has been so long since I have got any letters, but it is probable that changing regiments has been the cause of my losing some. Hereafter you will direct to me care of Capt. Geo. F. Y. Earle, Lawrence, Ks., and I shall probably get them. Please write soon and let me know all about Charles. How is Mother's health now? My love to her and to my sisters with a good share for yourself.

Yours truly,

Geo. W. Packard

Camp Pike, near Ft. Larned

July 4, 1862

Dear Bro. Zibeon,

I have just arrived here after a forced march of 300 miles, travelling from 35 to 50 miles a day. I am in good health and fine spirits. We start tomorrow for Fort Lyon a distance of 250 miles, but shall not make a forced march.

I was at Aunt Sarah's before I started on the trip. They were all well and awful glad to see me. Had a furlow for 5 days. We have the best behaved and drilled company in Kansas. Nothing I hate worse than a rabble of uncouth greenhorns that call themselves volunteers.

I want to hear from home as soon as I can, and never write without telling me all about Charles for he has always had a chance to be at the brunt of the war.

I have no more time to write now and please excuse this short letter and will try to [be] longer next time.

Please direct to me in care of Capt. Geo Earl, Co A 9 Reg K Vol. Ft Lyon.

Yours truly,

G. W. Packard

Tony Allen

Fort Riley, Kans.

Aug. 15, 1862

Dear Brother Zibeon,

Well here I am back again on my old stomping ground after march over twelve hundred miles. My health is good and would gladly march twenty five hundred more miles to get to Richmond. But hardly expect such a good opportunity to help crush the rebellion.

Not a word have I heard from home since I started on this trip and I am almost disheartened in regard to ever hearing from home again or from Charles. But I intend to keep writing home for a year or two more and then if I don't hear from you I shall give you up for lost and look me up a wife to see if she won't supply the place.

Fort Riley is the prettiest fort in the country. All of stone of the nicest kind finely planned and a beautiful parade ground situated at the head of the Kansas River, on the junction of the Smokey Hill and the Republican rivers. Good water, good climate and very healthy.

People are becoming frightened about drafting. I long to see a lot of the proslavery hounds in Kansas taken into the army. I think we can do them good and it will purify the atmosphere along the border of Mo.

I want you to write to me as soon as you get this letter and give me all the news about home and all about Charles and tell him where to write to me. Please direct to me, Co A 9th Reg. K. Vs. Ft. Riley, Kansas

My best love to all my folks, My best love to all my folks,

Yours truly,

Geo. W. Packard

Fort Scott, K. T.

Oct. 1, 1862

Dear Mother,

I just received a letter from you and one from Charles which has done me a great deal of good. The letters that you and Charles sent to Riley were forwarded to me by a friend. We are all in good health and spirits. Our company is now a body-guard for Gen. Blunt, which is a good position. It has the reputation of being the best company in the western department. We have 101 men for duty. It looks like a regiment in comparison with some of the Kansas regiments. We start this evening with the Gen. For some part of Mo., but don't know where. I think the prospect looks better for our country than it has for some time and look for the war to be stopped in six months, I hope that it will.

I was glad to hear that Chas. has got home safely but sorry to learn that he was in poor health. I will try to write him in a few days. I hardly thought that Zibeon would get into the service but if he thought it was his duty to go, he is not the man to stay at home.

The boys are all in a bluster all around me and I shall have to close. I send a daguerreotype in this letter. It is a poor picture, too dark.

My love to you all,

Yours truly,

Geo. W. Packard

Please direct to me Co. A 9 Reg. K Vs. Ft. Scott [and oblige]

Tony Allen

Ft. Scott

Feb 8th, 1863

Dear Sister Hannah,

As it is wet without and I have nothing to do, I will try and pen you a line or two. I am still trying to help get my country out of trouble but it is a hard job and I have a good notion to let Uncle Sam take care of himself. If he gets into a scrap again I shall let him get out of it the best way he can. Patriotism is a good thing but bumming around all over the worst part of the country, camping out in the snow, marching in the cold and storms, hunting [Bushwhackers*] will freeze out the patriotism of any true Americans. I hope that my patriotism will thaw out when warm weather comes, for I still believe in the Union.

It has been some time since I have heard from home or from either of my brothers in the army. I hope they are well for health is a great thing in the army.

I hope you and Mother, Wm., Elizabeth and Ella and Lizzy, Zibeon's wife and child are all well and in good spirits.

I should like to slip in to see you and after talking awhile, take supper with you for I presume you have butter, cheese, apples, etc. We would talk a while and then would have a bit of apples out of the cellar and then why,--I should sleep in a good bed. Don't you think I should be as happy as a man could be on this earth.

I hope to enjoy that privilege after the war is over and hope to meet you all with Zibeon and Chas. Excuse that bad written letter, for one in a tent with a dozen cutting all manner of antics, and sitting on the ground with paper on his lap is not in the most favorable mode of writing. Please write often.

My regards to all the folks,

Yours truly,

G. W. Packard

[*Confederate Guerilla during Civil War. Added by Tony Allen from Encarta Encyclopedia.]

Tony Allen

Paola, Kansas

May 7, 1863

Dear Bro. Zibeon,

I received a letter from you last eve, and was very glad to hear from you to learn that you are alive and well. You have sacrificed more than either of your brothers for your country, for you had a wife and little one to part with, which no doubt was hard. I trust you will be rewarded for all you suffer for your country.

The indications are good for a speedy termination of the war. Gen. Hooker is doing well. We shall hear favorable news soon from Vicksburg. The next attack on Charleston will result in the taking of it (so says my best judgment.)

The prospects for the success of our armies was never so flattering as at the present time.

Starvation, grim starvation is now staring them in the face, and that is man's most terrible enemy. Who can but pity the poor women and innocent children, but it is none too good for traitors.

Our reg. is stationed along the line to protect our settlements from the bushwhackers. Murder, robbery, and plunder seem to be the order of the day. But the 7th Kansas is a terror to them. We are all well mounted and when we set on their trail our Galigers patent rifles and Colts Dragoon revolvers are apt to talk in a thundering tone to them. You can hardly imagine the amount of traveling I have done through the brush in Arkansas and Mo. for them.

I presume that you will have a chance to give the Rebs one or two shots before you go home. Not that I am anxious to have you get into danger but conclude that you are anxious to do it.

We had a heavy frost here last night. It probably has done much damage, but think that we should have a good "crop" season this year.

I intend to go home after the war is over, but it will not be the young "fop" that left there six years ago. The change has been great probably on all of us. I am a western man all over, but don't think that it an improvement by any means. Please direct Co. A. 7th Reg.K.Vs Paola, Ks.

With much love I close.

Yours truly

Geo. W. Packard

(write soon)

Tony Allen

Paola, Kansas

June 27, 1863

Dear Brother,

As I have an opportunity this morning, I will try and write you a line.

I have been at work most of the time for weeks scouting after bushwhackers. About two weeks ago a party of about fifty men belonging to our regiment were surprised by a gang of double their number of bushwhackers. They were in a lane when attacked and were followed up through the lane for about one mile, when our men formed a line of battle and the bushwhackers fled, falling back through the lane shooting through the head all the wounded soldiers (14 in all). Not one of the fourteen but what were shot in the head, six more were badly wounded but hid from them.

Our party of about the same number went through the lane about three hours ahead of them on our way to Kansas City, five miles distance. On hearing of the disaster, we were on the field on double-quick. We hunted the country over, picked up the killed and wounded all that night. The next morning we struck a trail and followed it through the brush so thick that one could hardly get along, until about noon, we saw horses ahead, dismounting, we crept on our hands and feet until we were almost among them when we found there were only five of them with all of the horses and plunder they had found and taken the day before. We dispatched four of them and the fifth escaped, but without arms. We captured all of their plunder which consisted of about 16 horses, 9 revolvers and about the same number of guns, etc.

Our Co. has never been surprised by them for the fact that we are always on the alert, we never move without an advance man has his gun ready for use. We have adopted their rule, is to take no prisoners, leave no wounded men. There is no other way to fight bushwhackers. Extermination is our motto. We hunt them like wolves and are fast ridding the country of them.

I am well and in good spirits. Live well in private family when here and when out make the secesh (sp?) women cook for us.

I am well satisfied with the raids that the Rebels are making into Pen. and Ind. They will injure copperheads** more than anyone else. I regard it as the saving of our country for the copperheads are very bold in these states.

I hope to hear from you soon. My love to all.

Yours truly,

George W. Packard

[**Copperheads (political party), name popularly applied during the American Civil War to Northern members of the Democratic Party, also known as Peace Democrats, who opposed the administration of Abraham Lincoln and advocated compromise with the Confederate states to end the war. Not all those called Copperheads, however, were sympathetic to the Southern position in the war. Many objected to a vigorous prosecution of the war on the grounds that the conquest of the South was illegal or impossible. The most conspicuous Copperhead was Ohio Congressman Clement Laird Vallandigham, who was convicted of defying a military order that forbade any declaration of sympathy with the South and was banished to the Confederacy. The derivation of the name is uncertain; it may have referred either to the copperhead snake or to buttons cut from the copper coins depicting the goddess of liberty that were worn by many Peace Democrats. --- Definition added by Tony Allen from Encarta Encyclopedia.]

Tony Allen

Ft. Scott, Kansas,

July 22, 1863

Dear Mother,

It has been some time since I have written home but it is not because I have not wanted to. I have been mostly all over Ark., Cherokee Nation, Mo. And am now up in Kansas. I have come back to the 9th K. The Indians were deserting very fast and from the appearance of things I concluded that the regiment would not last long so I concluded to slip out when I could. My health is tolerable good. Got a bad cold and diarrhea but don't mind it much. We have had a very fine winter for the most part, very warm, have not had but four or five days any way uncomfortable to ride a horse back. Our Kansas troops have done more to crush out rebellion in the southwest than all the rest of the troops in the S.W.

It is probable that we shall stay in Kansas for a while in order to recruit ourselves and horses, for we have had a hard winter camping. I don't want to stay in this place for it is the worst part of K. I should like to spend the winter at home.

I want to hear from Zibeon and Charles and when you write, tell me all about them. If everybody was as anxious to have the war end as I am, I am certain that there would be a wind up seen, if some kind.

My love to you all, I still intend to come home when the war is over. Hope to meet all of you then. You will direct as usual. Co. A 9th Reg K. V. Ft. Scott, Kansas. Please write as soon as you get this or get some of our folks to write.

Yours truly

Geo. W. Packard

My Common, Remarkable Family

Little Rock, Ark

Oct. 4, 1864

Dear Bro. Zibeon,

I am, as you see by the date, still in Ark, although I have served out my three years.

The mustering officer musters no one out until three years from the completion of their company's organization. In my case it will be the 24th of this month. I had been hoping that I would be out on the 13th of last month for I wanted to get to Kansas for they are threatened both by hostile Indians and Rebs. I like it not to stay here under a Reb Gen. for such we believe Gen. Steel.

We have now in the Department sixty thousand troops doing nothing but guarding rebel towns and rebel property, but they find Kansas troops poor guards for rebel property. I don't know when I shall get home, but still think I shall make it this fall or the first of the winter.

I have been looking for letters from home for some time but they don't come, I have not had a letter from Chas for a long time. I think my letters have failed to reach him.

I think our prospects are better than they ever have been before for the termination of the war. Old Abe is the man.

Will little Mc' get any votes this fall in old Hebron. If so, I hope but scattering, for I think him no better than the party that nominated him and would carry out their platform if elected (if there is any platform to that balderdash they send forth.)

I have been having the ague and jaundice, diarrhea etc. for a month or so but am now on duty, shall probably have the ague more or less all the fall but it don't affect me as bad as it used to.

I want you to write to me in a week or two after getting this and direct it to Indianola, Kansas as I think I shall be there by that time. Be sure and write for I want to hear from home as soon as I get to Kansas.

Give my love to all inquiring friends and especially to Mother and Sisters with a good share for yourself and wife.

Yours truly,

George W. Packard

My Common, Remarkable Family

Indianola, Kansas

February 15, 1865

Dear Mother,

As I have an opportunity, I will write you a line. I have been looking for a letter from home for some time, but it don't come. Since I came up to Indianola I have written near twenty letters and have not got one in reply. I shall try and find new correspondents soon in order to hear from home once in a while. You must not think I am whipping you for you have written oftener than all the rest.

Our friends here are all well as usual. Last Sunday week I heard the Rev. S.D Bowker preach in Topeka, and it was one of the best sermons I ever heard in Kansas.

His health has improved since he came to K. but he ought not to try to preach. He started yesterday for Washington D.C. for the purpose of raising money to endow a College in Topeka. He will go all through the East. If perchance he goes to Hebron, he will call to see you.

We have had but little snow this winter for the most part warm and pleasant.

I hope you are all well at home. I am anxious to hear from Charles.

I have to write short letters as I don't have much to write, and my mind is too muddy to enter into a long dissertation on any of the thrilling topics of the day and so if I write enough to satisfy you that I am still "groveling here below" and in tolerable health, you must not expect more.

My love to all, hope to hear from home soon.

Yours truly,

George W. Packard

Tony Allen

Trenton N.J.

August 6th, 1865

Dear Brother,

Yours of the 30th is at hand. Was glad to hear from home for it was the first that I had heard since I left. I had a letter from Charles the other day. He has sent in his resignation and I think he will be home soon.

He has got the ague and I think it will shake some of this ideas that he has about the care of chills and fever out of him, but I am sorry that he has got it.

The N. J. troops are nearly all mustered out and I think we shall have tolerable good times. I don't think we shall be here long althow* there is no talk of our leaving yet. We were payed* off the other day. There is an abundance of peaches, tomatoes, potatoes etc. and very cheap so we can live well or something like white men with but little extry* expence.

The people here seem friendly and obliging althow there are a great many copperheads. Those that are true are as good friend as a soldier need have.

We are not confined so close to camp as we were when we first came here.

It affords me great pleasure to think of the great happy days I spend at home, and I wish it were so that I could spend my life in old Hebron or where I could see my friends often. But I have made Kansas my home, and I think it my duty to stay there, and I think when I get back there and take to myself a wife I shall be happy, and contented.

I long for the time to come when I shall get out of the army so that I can go home again and then go back to Kansas. But I try to be contented and think it the easiest way.

I should be glad to have you write me a regular family letter, have Mother write some and your wife some. I know you don't have much time to write but I think among you all you can write me three pages.

Remember me to all the neighbors. Kiss the children for me. And may the best of Heavens blessing be showered down upon you all is the prayer of your unworthy brother.

Truly yours

Geo. W. Packard

*actual spelling of Geo W Packard

Tony Allen

Harts Island, N Y

Aug 13, 1865

Dear Brother

Yours of the 4th inst is at hand. Was glad to hear that you was out of the army and I hope that before this you are at home.

Our Regt left Trenton day before yesterday and arrived here the next day. We are on a small island about three miles long and about 20 miles from N Y City in Long Island Sound, banished as completely as ever Napoleon was, however it matters but little where a fellow soldiers as long as they give him his grub and don't work him too hard. Mules, horses and soldiers can feel contented if well fed, but enough of this for I am as well contented here as I was in Trenton.

I take it for granted that you are at home as happy as mortal man can be. Well, I don't begrudge you your happiness but I do wish that I was there to enjoy it with you. You wish to know how I know that Miss D expects to be Mrs. P. Well, I want you to understand that I have not been over the world for nothing altogether. I have learned to read the signs of the times and seldom make a mistake and think I did not in the case of Miss D.

Give my love to Mother and all the family.

Please direct to Co. G. 8th. Reg U.S.v.v. Hart's Island, New York.

Write soon.

Yours truly,

George

Harts Island

Aug 13, 1865

Dear Mother,

As I have an opportunity I will try and write you a line.

I have made two moves since I left home and should be glad to make another but as now we occupy the worst place on the globe. I think we shall be obliged to stay. I try to be contented and think I succeed tolerable well. If I was not contented I should be sick, I am sure, for nearly half of the Reg't are on the sick list but I think that as soon as they get used to the water they will get better.

I need not express to you the amount of pleasure that my visit gave me. It was not a pleasure of but the short time I spent with you but it is a continuing pleasure and I trust a lasting benefit, and when I look forward to the time when I shall again see you, what joy and hope it gives me.

I think that a man that lives a life of monotony can have but little idea of the pleasures that one has who subjects himself to all the ills and dangers of life for the good of his country and his fellowman, and then reaps the reward of an approving conscience and the approval and welcome of his friends.

I think that I have a great deal to be thankful for, for the preservation of life, for health, and for so many friends and the pleasure of meeting them. I find it a great deal easier for me when I look at the many blessing I receive and try to be thankful for them, than to look at the dark side of the picture or feel that life does not go right. And then there is the hope that we shall after this life enjoy the presence of God and where we shall not be separated for a term of years or months.

I am anxious to hear from home as I have not had but one letter since I left there, to know that you are all well and to know how Hannah is. My

Tony Allen

love to all.

Direct to Harts Island N. Y.

Truly yours from your unworthy son

George

Washington D.C.

Oct. 19, 1865

Dear Brother

You will see by my caption that I have moved again. We came here from N.Y. by water in a steam transport. Were four days coming. I stood the trip well but we had tolerable rough usage on the boat for it was not capable of carrying half the men that was on her, without putting them to a good deal of inconvenience.

We are in quarters within two hundred yards of the State House. Duty here is not hard and we have enough to eat which we did not have on Hart Island. I have not heard from home for some time. I sometimes think that I shal* gett* home before New Year, and have nothing to encourage that belief with the exception that they are mustering out a good many one year men.

I should like much to spend the winter with you. I hope that mother is well. Charles' prospects seem to be very good. Have had one letter from him since he went to Portland.

You must excuse a short letter this time as I have but little time to myself today. Write soon.

Yours truly,

George

[* his spelling]

Tony Allen

Washington D. C.

Dec 7th 1865

Dear Mother,

As this is Thanksgiving Day, I know of no better way for me to spend an hour than in writing to you.

How I wish I could be with you today. But as that is out of the question lett* me try to be thankful for life and its many blessings, that war is no longer raging in our midst and that none of us have been victims to the terrible conflict that is at an end, that slavery has come to an end. As I think the black man should be thankful today as well as white.

I did hope that I might go home by this time as at Christmas, but have no hope of it now. In a little over three months my time will be out and then I hope to be with you.

Our prospects are good for getting that bounty that was stolen from us as we have secured the influence of Gen. Hancock and of several influential statesmen and if a bill passes to equalize the bounties, giving additional bounties to the '61 soldiers, and I have no doubt but it will, I shal* come under its provision, so you see I am hopeful. Such windfalls would help me to make a start in the world after getting out of the army.

It seems to me that it would have been better for all hands if you had left Hannah (poor girl) at Augusta. Yett* I know why she was taken home. You still hoped that she might be restored to reason and even if not you would have the consciousness that all had been done that could be.

May God help you to bare up under all your trials. I would that I could make your task liter*.

I hope to hear from you soon. Your letters are always so good and full of a mother's kindness and affection that I love to gett* them.

With much love to you all, I close.

Yours truly

George

[*his spelling]

[George Washington Packard is finished with his service and married to Georgiana Packard.]

Topeka, Kansas

Aug.26, 1866

Dear Mother,

As Georgie has written a sheet and wants me to contribute, I will try cheerfully. How often I think of you and home and regret that we are so far apart yet as I have voluntarily come so far from you to live, I must try to make the best of it and not complain. I have many good friends here and always expect to have wherever I am.

We have Congregational preaching here half the time, and a very good preacher he is too. Have prayer meetings every Sunday evening. We have but few to take part in our meetings yet they are very interesting and I hope useful.

I wish that I could be of more use in the meetings. At best we are weak here but we hope that God will add unto the church here of such as shall be saved. I am trying to live a Christian life and to walk in the fear of God. It is a great help to me to have a Christian wife to help me in the path of duty and rectitude, I have to mourn over my past life a great deal, for I have come short of living as I should, but by the help of God I shall try in the future to a better life.

Georgie is quite unwell and has fever for a number of weeks. I hope that she will be better soon altho she may be unwell for a long time.

My hands bothered me a great deal this summer. It is almost impossible to get them toughened to hard work, but I expect they will have to come to it.

Remember me to all the family and to all who may inquire after me. Give Ida and Bertha each a kiss for me (how I want to see them). May God bless you for all that you have done for your children and may God help us to meet you in heaven.

With much love, I remain your son,

George

Tony Allen

Leon, Kans

July 24, 1867

Dear Brother,

A letter from you and the girls reminded me that I have been delinquent in writing you. It was with deep regret that I learned of the death of sister E. She was a good woman, a good sister, and loving wife and mother. She has (passed) to her reward and her good influence will long out live her memory. We, too, remain on the downhill side of life. I feel, for one, that I should "set my house in order". I wish to leave my family in a comfortable condition and then my mission is ended.

We are in the midst of a terrible drought. I have 40 acres of corn and can never make ten bushel to the acre, over three acres of potatoes ruined, ten acres of oats that were not worth cutting, the pasture all dried up, a thing that has never happened before since I lived here, garden ruined and shade trees dying. Have not had but one good rain this spring or summer, and that not half what we needed at the time and that was over three weeks ago. It is not so over all the state but spotted some localities have had enough rain. The heat is intense, the thermometer runs over a hundred every day.

I am digging a well, have struck water, think I shall have enough for all purposes. Well it looks rather dark for me, had but little better than half crop last year on account of drought. I would sell and leave here but can't sell. If I could I should go to S.West Louisiana where it rains and where it is not so hot as it is here (don't laugh) for it is so, it never gets above 90F near the gulf.

Some of our neighbors are going soon. "A rolling stone etc." Well when one finds he is not doing well, he had better change with a chance to better himself. Stock cannot be raised here only at a loss. Eastern syndicates monopolized the business and ruined the western farmer. Our railroads are all owned in the east and we are paying them interest at three thousand dollars a mile besides that we have given them.

Three fourths of the farms of the west are mortgaged to eastern? and the towns are still worse off. Now what is the matter! We are paying 42 percent tariff on all manufactured goods whether imported or manufactured at home. Now 77 per cent of our exports are the product of agriculture, the price of which (you know) is regulated in Liverpool, the world's market. The price of surplus regulates the price of the whole, hence we get what it is worth to ship to Liverpool. Now should a farmer be a protectionist or rather should the west stand an institution that is robbing them.

[This was the end of the first page and cannot find page 2. There is no signature but I am sure it is George W. Packard. Ruth Allen]

Tony Allen

Eldorado, Butler Co.

Oct 39, 1870

Dear Mother,

It has been a long time since we have written to you, but hope you will pardon us for our seeming neglect. We broke up housekeeping in April in Lawrence and have been moving and getting ready to live down here [about one hundred and twenty miles S. W of Topeka] and we were eight days on the road. It rained nearly all the time. You can imagine that we had a tough time camping out, for we had to most of the time. We arrived here pretty well tired out but none of us sick which we have reason to be thankful for.

In the summer, Edith showed signs of being near sighted as we supposed, but did not feel much uneasy about her until we had been here a few days, we found that she could not see scarcely anything with her left eye and but poorly with her other. It has caused us a great deal of uneasiness about her. I wrote to Charles a full description as near as I could of her case, and hope to hear from him soon. We wrote to Lawrence to get Dr Morris' opinions about it and to get opinions from other physicians there. Dr Morris sent a prescription which is intended for doctoring her blood. Have not had a chance to try the medicine yet. Another physician thought it might be a cataract, but I don't think it is for the film that came over the sight seems to be in the center of the eye.

I have taken a claim here and like the country first rate. Climate is warm, making it an excellent stock country. We dug two hills of potatoes the other day, yielded a large wooded pail full, or six hills to the bushel. There were excellent crops of wheat, oats and corn. Everything that has been plowed here this year has produced an excellent crop. Should like to have some of my down east friends come and settle near me. It seems some out of the world here yet, but it will be but a short time until we have the iron horse as near or nearer than we should want it.

I took quite a colony here with me, Wm Jordan, Samuel Packard, C.Plummer. I am in partnership with Plummer for the present.

Little Florence is well and fat as butter and not half the trouble that poor Edith is. We milk five cows now and Georgie is making lots of butter which will sell for fifty cents per lb.

Hope to hear from you soon and will try to write to you oftener. Remember us to all our folks, want to see you all very much.

With much love, I remain, your

George

Unknown location, probably Leon or El Dorado Kansas

Probably early 1870s

Brother Zibeon,

As Georgie is writing to mother I will try to write you a line. I find it nearly impossible to write any as my time is all taken up opening a farm when in the house the babies demand my attention.

I shall in three or four days have 15 acres of ground broke, have 10 in corn [?] a part of which looks well and a part of it was broke the wrong time of the year and is very grassy and chokes the corn. Shall have roasting ears in about a week.

I have about twenty acres fenced in, and have built about one hundred rods of post and rail fence this spring, and just as I got it done a terrible gale rocked it all over a good deal, but tore down but little of it. I did not get served near as bad as most of my neighbors did as nearly all the fence in this neighborhood was blown down, and a good many houses and we must have been very near the center of the storm. The climate here is rather hot for me and in fact I am fearful that out of doors work in this hot climate will not do for me.

I hope to hear from you as often as you can write.

With love to all,

George

[no town or date, Probably Lawrence in January 1872 Ruth Allen}

Dear Mother,

I will try to write you a line in addition to what Georgie has written. Edith don't want me to write or read while at home, so I hardly write any at all. Our children are a great comfort to us. And if they were someone else's they would be a great deal of trouble, but as it is they are no trouble at all, of course.

We are getting along as well as expected.

Don't know what will turn up, trade is very dull. I wish we were not so far apart for I am such a poor writer that I don't like to undertake it at all but if I was near enough to see you as often as the rest of your children can, I should be glad and I wish you could see our children.

I hope the time will come when I can take my family east on a visit, but if we succeed in having children for the next ten years as fast as for the two past years, I think our chances will be slim.

I think that you keep up remarkably well under all the circumstances. Poor Hannah, how I wish she would get well. I am glad that Charles has taken a wife. Have no doubt she will prove a great blessing to him. Think his prospects are good now. Zibeon, it is to be presumed, moves on in the "even tenor of his way" "happy as a big sunflower" and Ellen, ditto.

I want to see all of you very much, and by the way, you just charter a car and come out and see us. I will have the Eldridge House ready for you any time, just say you will come.

And now as it is not far into January, I wish you all a happy new year and may God's blessing rest down upon you, is the prayer of your son,

George

Tony Allen

Lawrence, Kans

May 11, 1872

Dear Mother,

It has been a long time since we heard from you or you from us. I hardly known what to write. We waited a long time for your grandson to make his appearance so that we could send you the good news, and then I went south to "enter" or pay for my place. Then we began to see some change in Etith's eyes so we have been watching and waiting, and I can now say to you with a glad heart that her eyes are getting better. The spots are going off very fast and we have hope that she will have good eyes, but do not hope too much.

We had a great deal of sickness while south and I began to fear that we should lose both children and perhaps ourselves altogether if I stayed there so I packed up and came back to Lawrence. Edith has been sick a great deal since we got back and was near dying in Topeka on our way up here, but her health now seems to be better than it has for a long time. We hope to hear the next time we hear from you that your health is entirely restored. I have often thought of you. I think that you must have suffered so much during your long fever. I want to see you all very much but don't know when I ever shall. Only such as can come out here to see us. I should like to have Zibeon come out to see the country this summer. I think there is to be an excursion out and back from Boston this summer for thirty dollars the round trip.

Remember me to all of our folks. Hope to hear from you soon.

With much love,

George

5 ADDENDOM I

GEORGIANA AND GEORGE WASHINGTON PACKARD PHOTOS AND INFORMATION

Monson, Maine Childhood home of Georgiana Packard

Hebron, Maine Home of George Washington Packard before his relocation to Kansas

Hebron Academy

Hebron Academy, founded in 1804, is a small, independent, college preparatory boarding and day school for boys and girls in grades six through postgraduate. At Hebron students from across the United States and around the world are challenged and inspired to reach their highest potential in mind, body, and spirit through small classes, knowledgeable and caring teachers who provide individual attention, and a friendly, respectful, family atmosphere.

1804 - Charter granted by the General Court of Massachusetts on February 10.

1805 - William Barrows, Jr. opens the Academy on September 3.

1807 - Weekly tuition set at 20 cents, reduced from the original fee of 25 cents.

1808 - With 60-70 volumes, the town's secret Tryocinic Adelphi Society forms a library.

1814 - Deacon Barrows' house burns on December 14. Lost in the fire were the treasurer's records and the original records of the Tyrocinic Adelphi Society.

1819 - The Academy building burns. In his "little ewe lamb" speech, Deacon Barrows successfully thwarts a plan to move the school to Paris Hill.

1821 - New Academy building is ready for use.

1826-27 - Hannibal Hamlin, later Lincoln's Vice President, attends Hebron.

1829 - Trustee House is built about where Atwood Hall is today. It serves as the preceptor's house and as a dormitory.

1837 - Deacon Barrows dies. He served as a trustee for 33 years.

1844-1845 - The school catalog lists 55 students for the fall term and 106 for the spring. The terms were 20 weeks long, with a four-week summer vacation and an eight-week winter break.

1847 - The third Academy building is erected. It is a two-storey brick building with a tower and belfry rising in front

Hebron Maine Homestead where George Washington Packard grew up. Homesteaded by Reuben Packard 1796.

Topeka, Kansas Destination of Cyrus Packard and his family

Quito, Kansas Homestead location of George Washington and Georgiana Packard when their children were young

Older six children of George Washington and Georgiana Packard. Back Row left: Raymond, Edith, Fred. Front Row left: Ida, Mable and Florence. A funny note: In her 1870 letter Georgiana referred to Florence as a "mischievous imp" and about the same time George Washington referred to her as; "Little Florence is well and fat as butter and not half the trouble that poor Edith is." Photo is about 1888.

Three younger children of Georgiana and George Washington Packard, from the left: Maud, Muriel and Arthur Grant about 1888.

My Common, Remarkable Family

Georgiana and George Washington Packard Family: Back Row from left: Maude Grace, Arthur Grant, Ida Faye, Frederick William (blind), Florence Nightengale, Edith Longfellow (very poor eyesight). Front Row from left; Raymond Barrows, Mabel Claire (blind), George Washington, Georgiana, Muriel Joy. Unfortunately this is from a Xerox copy.

George Washington Packard

Packard Sisters in Topeka, Kansas, back row from the left, Olive and Georgiana, front row left Hannah and Sarah on the right

Older Georgiana on the left and Olive on the right

Bill Passed by the U.S. Senate to Increase Georgiana's Veteran's Pension from $12 to $24

Georgiana Packard – Bill to increase her pension from $12 to $24 per month

Pages 34 and 35

62o CONGRESS,

3d Session.

SENATE.

RETORT No. 1168.

PENSIONS AND INCREASE OF PENSIONS TO CERTAIN SOLDIERS AND SAILORS OF THE CIVIL WAR, ETC.

JANUARY 29, 1913.—Ordered to be printed.

Mr. McCuMBER, from the Committee on Pensions, submitted 7the

following

REPORT.

[To accompany S. 8314.]

This bill is a substitute for the following Senate bills referred to said committee:

S. 8173. Georgiana Packard is the widow of George W. Packard, who enlisted September 13. 1861, as a private in Company A. Ninth Kansas Cavalry, and was honorably discharged November 19. 1864. He again enlisted March 16.

1865. as corporal in Company G. Eighth United States Veteran Volunteers, and was mustered out March 15. 1866. He was a good soldier and has a highly creditable record. He died October 26, 1912, being at the time of his death a pensioner under the age and service act of May 11, 1912, at the pate of $30 per month.

Claimant was married to the soldier April 17. 1866. She is now receiving the pension of $12 per month provided by the act of April 19, 1908. to the widow of a soldier who served 90 days in the Civil War. It appears, however, that she is 67 years old. and evidence filed with th:s committee shows that she is in poor health and in very needy circumstances. She is physically unable to do any work and has no property except a small home and no other income than her pension. She has two children, both of whom are nearly blind and unable to do anything toward earning a living, and are dependent upon their mother for care and support. It is believed that the soldier's honorable and faithful service of four years and the widow's advanced age, poverty, and physical infirmities justify the committee in recommending increase of her pension to $24 per month to aid in the care and support of her afflicted children.

From the Congressional Serial Set – By the United States Printing Office

Gravestone of George Washington and Georgiana Packard at Rochester Cemetary near Topeka, Kansas

6 MY REFLECTIONS BY RUTH PACKARD ALLEN

POEM BY FRED PACKARD TO HIS BROTHER ARTHUR ON THE BIRTH OF RUTH ELIZABETH PACKARD

To Arthur

Congratulations are due
Which I now offer you
For that girl of 8 pounds

And of course, it's my duty
To Say she's a beauty
Whether she can cry or laugh

Don't step so high
For I'm sure by-an-by
You will need some of that motion

For when she's grown up
Like a fine buttercup
She will have her vey own notion

Tony Allen

Now carry her so
And croon to her low
With songs not learned from a teacher

And she'll cuddle down
I'll bet my bald crown
And be the most cunning little creature

This one will require
A harp and a lyre,
And before long she'll be wanting a pearl

For she's not a boy
Nor will put up with their toy
But she is your own little girl

P.S. Just one other word,
I wonder if you heard
The stork when he came to your place?

For if you did see
That it was really he,
We could learn how to increase the race.

FRED

My Reflections

By Ruth Packard Allen

Preface

If on the following pages you find a few inaccuracies remember that I have called it "My Reflections". Reflections are apt to be slanted, so I hope you will forgive these minor (I hope) refractions.

My story covers many decades. I have tried to show the changes during each decade in news, styles, and family.

My Reflections

Georgiana Packard

I am a granddaughter of Georgiana Packard and am proud of the heritage which she and other forebears have given me. This segment of the ongoing saga covers a time span from around the turn of the century, when Georgiana's journal left us, to today, 1987.

The house where we visited my grandmother in Topeka was across the street from the Kansas State Fair Grounds. This was the last home in which she and Grandpa Packard had lived with their big family. Grandpa died five years before I was born, so I had no opportunity to know him. He was a Civil War soldier and served under General Grant. He had a personally autographed copy of Grant's Memoirs. It is understandable that he favored naming my father, Arthur Grant Packard. Arthur Grant was number seven in their family of nine children.

I cherish the few memories I have of Grandmother Georgiana. One of the most vivid was of her standing at the table in her country kitchen with its iron pump in the corner. She was rolling out cookies and winking at me. My feeble attempts to mimic her brought a merry, loving laugh from her. Another memory I have is of a visit to her home on a special occasion when all of the Packard Clan was gathered in the parlor. My aunts and grandmother fixed a play corner in the dining room where they had turned a train stool upside down for me to play in. They also let me play with a doll that had highly glazed china head, hands, and feet (little black, high top shoes). The body of the doll was of leather that had been stuffed.

Grandmother Georgiana must have been a terrific mother. She reared her large family without too much money, but they were a proud and happy group. Several of the children had visual handicaps and were unable to read (until they attended the Kansas State School for the blind and learned to read Braille). My father told of his mother's reading to her children each evening from the Bible, from her set of Dickens' novels, and from other classics.

As expenses mounted in this large family, those who could helped fill the coffers. The older girls taught school. My father was only able to have a fourth-grade formal education before he was apprenticed as a printer's helper. I have thought since, that perhaps he learned as much in reading skills in a print shop as he might have in school. However, he was not satisfied with the education he had, and continued for years with correspondence schools. I still have some of the books which he used as texts in grammar, mathematics, writing, and some engineering.

It was through his study that he was able to change jobs to building and architecture. He was building a roundhouse for the Santa Fe Railroad when he met a cute little brunette secretary, Golda Barr. They started dating and attended Euclid Avenue Methodist Church in Topeka, where the young people had an active social life. On September 1, 1906, they slipped off to Carbondale, Kansas, where an old friend of Arthur's married them. They did not tell of the secret marriage until Arthur's next job took him to Dodge City, Kansas. Golda wanted to go with him, so it had to be told. Their first child died at birth. After losing this little girl, they had three sons, George Stafford, Charles Everett, Eugene Lewis, and another daughter, Ruth Elizabeth. We were all born in Topeka.

-1920s -

Florella Barr (left) with her daughters and their beaus; Aaron Bishop, Sylvia Barr, Arthur Grant Packard, Golda Barr

News in the '20's was reported solely by newspaper. Kansas City had the K C Times (morning), K C Star (evening), K C Journal, and the K C Kansan.

The Times ran serials each day, which was kind of a forerunner of the soap operas of today. Ladies could look forward to reading a segment from a novel each day, of such authors as Faith Baldwin or Gene Stratton Porter. In the funny papers (comics), Skeezex was a baby who was left on the doorstep of bachelor, Walt Wallet in "Gasoline Alley". I have watched him grow up as I grew up, and he is now a grandfather as "Gasoline Alley" is still going on. The evening papers carried a story

Arthur and Golda Packard Wedding Picture

of Peter Rabbit which my mother read to me while I brushed her long hair.

The news was of a nation returning to normal following World War I. In 1927 Charles Lindberg made his solo flight across the Atlantic. In 1929 the Graf Zeppelin was the first and only Air Ship to go around the world.

Styles in the early '20s were very conservative. Ladies dresses were almost floor length. They always wore a corset, bloomers, petticoat, cotton stockings (usually black) and high-topped shoes. The only concession to hot weather was in using lighter material for dresses. Their hair was long and usually wound into a bun on top of the head. Hats were held on with a long hat pin which stuck through the hat and hair bun. Later in the 20's came the flappers-wow!

Men dressed in three-piece suits. The vest had two pockets. A watch was put in one pocket and a connecting chain draped across to the other pocket. Shirts were white with detachable collars, so that the shirt could be worn a second day with a fresh collar. Their basics included BVDs, socks held up with garters, high-top shoes, and flat straw hats in summer. Men of distinction wore spats.

Nightshirts were worn to bed. Glasses for both men and women were very small, frameless with fine gold ear pieces. Boys wore knickers until they were about twelve years old. When they graduated to long pants, they had a new status among their peers. Many boys begged to be allowed to wear long trousers before "Mama" deemed it prudent that they should do so. Little girls wore knee-length, loose-fitting dresses with matching bloomers, cotton stockings, and high-top shoes. It was such fun buttoning shoes. A button hook was pushed through the buttonhole to pull through the round button. Babies wore long dresses, long petticoats, stockings pinned to their three-cornered flannel diapers, and booties.

I mentioned flappers earlier. They came along in the mid '20s and were quite shocking. First, the ladies cut their long hair; they called it getting their hair bobbed. Next, the hemline on dresses kept going up until it was above the knee and irregular hemlines were in vogue. Dresses were straight and unbelted. Black cotton stockings were replaced by silk stockings with a seam up the back, and, oh what misery it was trying to keep that seam straight!

In 1920, Arthur was offered the job of branch manager of the Kansas Fire Inspection Bureau in Kansas City, Kansas. So the family packed up and left Topeka. The only house available for rent was in the Quindaro district. It had no central heating, running water, electricity, or indoor plumbing. Many cold trips were made to the outhouse, and Saturday-night baths were taken in a washtub in the dining room in front of the coal stove. Water was brought from a well a half-block away.

Ruth Packard about three years old

On wash days, Golda heated water in a large copper boiler on the wood stove. The washing machine was like a short, wood boat which was pulled out into the kitchen. (I guess you could not call it a machine, as the only moving parts were my mother's arms as she pushed the clothes back and forth with a wooden blade). She used a long wooden paddle to lift the clothes from the boiler. Extra dirty things needed to be scrubbed by hand on a washboard with soap made with cooking fat and lye. Golda usually had supper cooking on the back of the stove. On washday it was a large pot of ham and beans which was served with cornbread.

If washday seemed a chore, ironing day was even worse, especially in the summer. Flat irons needed to be heated on the wood stove and the kitchen got very hot without even an electric fan to help. Everything had to be ironed in those days, and many of them were starched.

Even with the inconveniences, this was a fun place to live. Golda's sister, Sylvia Bishop, and her four children were frequent visitors. Stafford and Dale Bishop were real buddies, but they shared their fun times with Charles and Gene. John Bishop and Ruth were good playmates and even allowed baby Howard Bishop to play with them occasionally. To Ruth, her cousin, Doris Bishop, seemed the ultimate in beauty and she could make the neatest paper dolls.

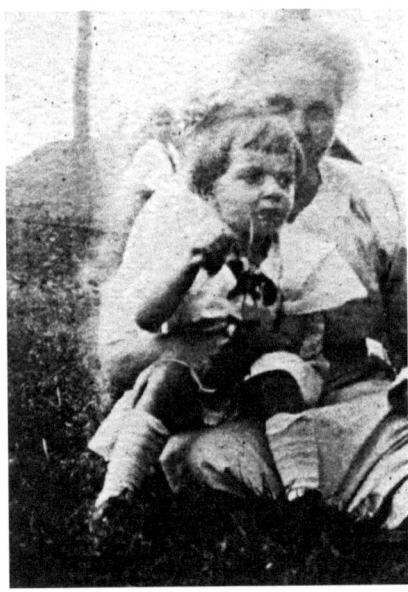

Ruth on Grandmother Florella Barr's lap

Grandmother Florella Barr, Golda and Sylvia's mother, left Argos, Indiana and came to live with Sylvia and Aaron Bishop. She visited us at one time and left a sweet memory. She and Grandmother Packard died in the early 1920s. My brothers probably remember our grandmothers better than I. (Our Grandfather, John Barr, died before I was born).

I wish Grandmother Georgiana might have been with us on Sunday afternoons as we hiked to the Quindaro Ruins. This was an area on the Missouri River where the Delaware Indians lived and where Grandmother's family had ended their river trip after coming from Maine to Kansas.

We were members of Quindaro Methodist Episcopal Church and my brothers and I attended Quindaro school until 1924, when we moved to 1329 Greeley. This big old Victorian house had everything from stain-glass windows to an indoor bathroom. Among some of the other unbelievable luxuries were: central heating, electricity, natural gas, a telephone, garage, and a basement. Lighting for the room was from a single light bulb suspended on about a four-foot cord from the ceiling. The switch was at the light and not on the wall. When we ironed, the cord was attached to a plug screwed into the light socket.

Golda now had a Maytag washing machine, It was square, made of heavy grey metal, and stood on four legs. Its wringer swung from the washer to the two rinse tubs and finally wrung the clean clothes into a basket to be sorted, starched and taken to the yard for hanging. The night before washday, Golda had the big copper boiler on the gas burner in the basement where white clothes had a night's boiling to make them whiter.

Clothes' hanging was an art and a source of pride. The lines were strung from tree to tree and held up with clothes props. The white sheets had to be hung together, very evenly, then the towels, according to size and color. Shirts, dresses, underwear and stockings were also hung according to size. There was a real competition among the neighbor ladies, to see who could be the first one with her line up, the one with the neatest line, and the one with the whitest whites. No one admitted it, of course, but it was there, this pride. My mother had a funny expression for the way she hung clothes when she was in too much of a hurry for such meticulous organization on the line she said: "I'll just hang them sheet, shirt, and didie." (Didie was her word for diaper).

Afternoons saw the ladies taking down their sweet-smelling dry clothes, and folding them neatly into clothes baskets. The ropes were then removed from the trees, wrapped from hand to elbow until it was a neat hank that could be hung in the basement until next washday. The clothes were then sprinkled, rolled and stored for ironing the next day. The ladies would "freshen up", put supper on the stove and wait on the front-porch swing for their husbands to come home. (Wash days were always on Monday and ironing day was on Tuesday).

Central heat was provided by a coal-burning furnace in the basement. The large coal bin was kept full by the coal man who delivered coal to the side of the house where there was a little door that opened into the coal bin. He had a chute which went from the truck into the coal bin. It was a very dusty operation. The only entrance to the basement was from the outside the house where a large door was over the steps. It had to be laid back in order to descend the steps. Arthur had to build the coal fire, bank it at night, and remove ashes frequently.

Ruth and her brothers: From left: Stafford, Charles, Gene, and Ruth – 1924

The kitchen now held a Roper gas stove which gave a cooking fire with just the touch of a match, a sink with running water, and an ice box. The ice man came each day, checked the amount of ice needed by the card in the front window, picked up a cake of ice with his big tongs and put it in the icebox.

We now had a telephone. It was upright with a receiver hanging at its side. When one lifted the receiver, he heard: "Number please". He gave the operator the number and waited for her to ring it for him. Sometimes, he would hear: "I'm sorry, that line is busy."

A garage housed the company car which Arthur drove, a model T Ford and later a Model A Ford. They had running boards on the side which held luggage and a spare tire. Sundays found the family driving to the farm near Lawrence to visit Arthur's sister, Maude Eberhard and her husband, William. Stafford, Charles and Gene enjoyed being with their cousin, Everett, and Ruth considered her cousin, Georgiana, the nearest thing to a sister that she would ever have. The trips were sometimes quite an adventure. The roads were either dirt or gravel. Dirt roads were murder, especially when it rained. They were slippery and filled with ruts. Gravel roads threw the rocks up onto the car, broke windows and slashed tires. Curves were not so much curves as right-angle turns. Of course, at the speed one traveled on the narrow roads, it was no problem. My brothers used to speak of the ultimate speed as, "a-mile-a-minute".

Luggage was strapped onto the running board and more was tied on top of the car when we took our vacations to Lake Okoboji, Iowa. There were six of us in the car, but often we were accompanied by a friend of Golda's, Lydia Strobel, or a cousin; Everett, or Georgiana. When Arthur had to fix a flat tire, he took the tire off the wheel, fixed the inner tube, put it back into the tire and pumped it up by hand. He was a very patient man. We did have some great times at Lake Okoboji. It made for family memories that are very dear to all of us.

The old Victorian house had a large stairway with a decorative newel post. It was my Saturday job to dust the stairway. Although still a girl, I was required to wear a dust cap like all the ladies did when doing housework.

There was about a half-acre yard with a terrace in the back. The brothers made a neat city on the terrace. They had a reservoir at the top and piped water down the hill to the little village sprawled on the side of the "mountain". Their roads were set up like real mountain roads with switch backs and their little steel cars were pushed around as they sounded horns: "a-ooga, a-ooga". Girls' toys were dolls made with stuffed bodies and a sewed-on head with eyes that closed. We also had celluloid toys (forerunner of plastic), and paper dolls which could be found in the Delineator Magazine. My greatest joy was my roller skates, until one of my big brothers decided he needed the wheels for his scooter.

Halloween was a special holiday. It was celebrated with Aunt Sylvia's family. Parlor games were played and the evening ended with the black pot. This large iron pot held small gifts for everyone. Each gift had a string attached and this was extended outside the pot with names on the end of the strings. The pot was covered so the goodies could not be seen until we were told we could pull the strings. We found our names and pulled out our surprises. Fun!! It is now some sixty years later and we all remember the black pot. I have renewed the tradition with our grandchildren. The gifts are necessarily inexpensive, but not as much so as they were in the depression days.

The crash of 1929 was the beginning of many years of deprivation for Americans. Arthur was able to keep his job, but had to work a month without pay. This was minor compared to the many that were jobless and destitute. The bread lines were heartbreaking. When ragged men came to the door asking for food, they were never turned away hungry. We had no money for extras, but since everyone was in the same situation, it did not seem so serious. We made do with what we had. No one worried about wearing darned stockings, or not having a large wardrobe.

Herbert Hoover was president during the depression. Some of the popular songs were: "Mr. Herbert Hoover says that Now's the Time to Buy, so Let's Have Another Cup of Coffee, and Let's Have Another Piece of Pie", also: "It's only a Shanty in Old Shanty Town", and "Brother, Can You Spare a Dime?"

-1930s –

Our next rented house was a Queen Ann style at 1042 Haskell. While we were living here, two of my brothers met and married their life's partners. Stafford married Mary Harding who was a sweet, vivacious girl and Gene married Ruth Jones who was (and is) as nice as she is pretty. Charles waited a few years before finding Helen Thomas, a cute little artist at Hall Brothers (this was the former name of Hallmark Cards).

George Allen entered the picture at this time. We attended the Western Highlands Presbyterian Church which had a very active young peoples' group. Since we were still living through the depression and money was not available for entertainment, the group offered much cheap social life. There were parties at various houses and picnics in nearby parks (sometimes cut short by dust storms). It was at a picnic in Mary and Stafford's back yard where I first saw George.

Soon after I arrived, I became aware of this new fellow in the crowd who was handsome and fun loving. I had just graduated from high school and this was a college man ready for his senior year at KU! I was sure one of the older, prettier girls would catch his eye. However, he did not have a choice because our minister made the decision for him. He arranged to take us to a banquet without either knowing the other would be along. It was a happy evening and the beginning of our dating. George was the brother of Mary Geiger and had come to Kansas City to stay with her, find a job, and earn enough money to return to KU to finish his degree. He never went back! (George's mother had died when he was only thirteen years old. His father was a poor Methodist preacher, so George was on his own). We dated for four years in which time he took a Civil Service examination and started working at the post office. In the four years of our dating, I graduated from KCK Jr. College, went to KC Business College, and worked at the Art Institute.

Arthur and Golda were finally able to buy their own home at 724 N. 32nd St. This was too far for George to visit, as he had no car and there was no public transportation to this area, so he bought his first car, a 1935 Pontiac. This car was to take us on our honeymoon and bring all four of our baby sons home from the hospital.

Ruth in Outfit her Mother made for her Sr. Breakfast at Wyandotte High School, 1935

Transportation to Business College was by way of streetcars. The first one was about a half mile from our home. It was a little puddle jumper trolley that had just one track, as there was just one car. This took me to the transfer point where I got a regular streetcar. The ride was kind of scary as it went across the river on the outside rail of the viaduct and it looked as though there was nothing between the rider and the water below. I tried not to lean toward the outside. At the other end of the viaduct, the streetcar entered a tunnel. When it emerged, Voila! Kansas City, Missouri.

Dale and Altheda Bishop were going to the World's Fair in New York City and asked George and me to accompany them. I was all for getting married right away and going along, but George was a little more mature in his thinking and we declined. We decided to wait until February 2, 1940.

George and Ruth on a picnic date with Altheda Berkey, Clarence and Jackie Renee, Dale Bishop took the Photo

Golda and Arthur's family now had only two children left at home, Charles and me. Evenings at home were spent listening to the radio to such programs as "Amos and Andy", "Fibber McGee and Molly", "George Burns and Gracie Allen", "Jack Benny", and the "Hit Parade." The soap operas on radio were: "One Man's Family" and "Stella Dallas".

When I was getting my trousseau together, my mother bought me a fancy pair of blue satin, fur-trimmed Daniel Green slippers. While we were in the store, I bought her a pair of black Daniel Greens for

Christmas unbeknownst to her. Both boxes were stored on my closet shelf. One day, while I was at work, she decided to take a look at the pretty slippers. The box she opened held plain black slippers! She was so upset; she grabbed the box, hurried down to the streetcar and proceeded to storm over to Jones Store shoe department. She was highly indignant as she told them that she had bought beautiful blue satin slippers and they had given her these ugly things. They were very sorry and searched for another pair of blue satins, but to no avail. Since there was quite a difference in price, they refunded the price of the blue ones and apologized most profusely. She was still steaming when I got home and she told me the story. I had to laugh as I told her that she had returned her Christmas present and went in to get the blue slippers to show her. I never did hear what she did about the difference in the refund. I have a feeling that she might have been too embarrassed to do anything.

Franklyn Roosevelt had defeated Herbert Hoover in 1932 and a new era started. His New Deal gave jobs to the unemployed. The WPA paid Federal money for jobs on roads, public buildings, and parks. This was the beginning of Socialism in our country, and of people thinking the government owed them a living. Our system of free enterprise was threatened, but I was happy to see the bread lines go. The depression was fading into the past. President Roosevelt had been crippled by polio and spent much time in Warm Springs, GA., where he had the "baths". Eleanor was a very active first lady. She wrote a column, "My Day", which appeared in most daily papers. She helped the black people begin to get away from their slave image, Grandmother Georgiana would have been proud of her. Franklyn Roosevelt was to serve an unprecedented three full terms in office and had been elected for the fourth term, but he died before completing it.

Styles were becoming more sophisticated with dress hems below the knee. The corseted look of the '20's was out, but girdles were a necessity. The depression put an end to happy-go-lucky flapper days. Ladies in the 30's did find a new freedom in sportswear, wide legged trousers which they called pajamas (not to be confused with night wear, these were sport pajamas).

While we were still in the throes of the depression, news of the '30s was pretty grim. We began to read about Hitler's Nazi party and Mussolini's Fascist party. The armies of both dictators were marching through and claiming small European countries. Jews were hated and after being rounded up, they were sent to death camps by the Nazis. The American people were appalled, but could do nothing with the depression weighing so heavily on them. England and France entered the war with Germany and Italy.

-1940s –

News of the '40s was of the end of the depression, and of America entering World War II. The Jewish race survived despite the Nazi attempt at annihilation. Jews from all over the world went to Israel to start a new nation. The Arabs claimed they took some of their land and there has since been a great deal of unrest in the Middle East.

George and Ruth Allen wedding, Feb. 2, 1940

Styles were quite conservative once more. Materials were scarce, so styles were skimpy. Narrow skirts were worn with Eisenhower (waist length) jackets. My favorite style was a wedding dress made by my mother. It was a white-moiré-taffeta which had a short train and twelve-button sleeves.

Our honeymoon was in New Orleans during Mardi Gras. We drove on narrow icy roads. This was before Interstate highways. We had $100 to spend on the trip, so we could not afford hotels in New Orleans. We stayed with a friend of Mary Geiger's and paid her $10 for a two-night stay. A hotel would have cost $15 a night, with a minimum of three nights!! We returned to Kansas City, Missouri to start our happy home in a third- floor apartment at 37th and Summit. Our rent was $37.50 a month for a furnished, one-bedroom apartment. We moved after six months to a first floor, unfurnished apartment at 34th and Euclid. This was our address when George registered for the draft.

According to our income tax records, George's annual salary in 1940, as a substitute Railway Mail Clerk, was $2,199. We were pretty proud of ourselves as we had bought furniture, paid for a baby, and saved $100. Our baby, Charles Anthony, was born December 2, 1940, and George and I had to learn to be parents in a hurry. (Anthony Eden was Prime Minister of England at the time and I liked the name).

It was December 7, 1941 when Pearl Harbor was bombed by the Japanese. One tends to remember exactly where he was and what he was doing when something of this magnitude happens. On this date, I was sitting on the sofa, playing with baby Tony, when George turned on the radio to hear the announcement...President Roosevelt was telling of the attack and said we were at "wah."

So World War II had started. We not only were at war with Japan, but we joined our allies in Europe in an effort to stop Hitler. General Dwight Eisenhower was supreme commander of the European Theater and General Douglas MacArthur held the same command in the Pacific. The draft was suddenly a very real thing. We wondered when George's number might be called as we saw friends and relatives leaving for the service. Charles Packard enlisted in the Navy, and he and Helen spent the war years in Washington D C, only returning to Kansas City and civilian life a few days after the funeral of our mother in 1945. John and Howard Bishop enlisted in the Navy, also, and they both saw service overseas in the Pacific. George's number was not drawn until 1944 when the war was virtually over. He passed the physical, but was never called. What a relief!

George and Ruth in their apartment at 37th and Summit, 1940

Correspondence to our friends in the service was via V-Mail. Letters had to be written on special forms, and then photographed. The negatives were developed and a copy was delivered. This not only eliminated bulky mailing, but also made censuring easier.

We lived briefly in a duplex in the Parkwood district in Kansas City, Kansas. When Stafford had his stroke at age 32, Mary asked if we would help them by taking over their lease for the house at 1147 Rowland, KCK. They could then move in with her parents. We were happy to do so, especially since Edward and Willardean were in the same block. George and Edward worked evenings at the K C Mo. Post Office. Willardean and I sometimes went on the bus to meet them after work to have dinner at Fred Harvey's Restaurant in the Union Station. This was late at night, and we felt perfectly safe being out on the street!

Christmas Breakfast 1942: From left; Gene and Ruthie Packard sons Gene (Bud) and Bruce, Mary Packard, Ruth Allen, Stafford Packard, daughter Martha Packard, Golda Packard, Tony Allen, Arthur Packard, notice the ice box in the kitchen.

We had only lived here two years when our landlord died and his wife wanted her house back. There was absolutely no rental available as the country was at war and rents had been frozen. Property owners could be very selective and renters with children or pets found it very difficult to find a home. As the time approached for us to give up the house, and we had found nothing, my parents kindly offered to share their home with us. We moved in with our three-year-old Tony and the three of us had a few bitter-sweet years with my parents.

The war was to change the life style and economic structure completely in America. Women went to work in Bomber Plants. "Rosie the Riveter" was a popular song. Women began, for the first time, to taste the independence of working outside the home. Their pay checks looked pretty good as compared to the depression wages, which were all too fresh in everyone's memory. When the men came home again, there were two pay checks to help young couples get started. Wives discovered they could take maternity leave to have families and thus started the "Baby Boom."

On the home front, we were doing all we could to conserve materials which could be used in the war effort. Many items were rationed, such as: gasoline, tires, meat, butter, sugar, flour, and shoes. It was difficult to buy material, so dresses were made from flour sacks, which the flour companies had graciously printed in pretty colors and prints. There was a saying: "Fix it up, wear it out, and make it do, or do without". We had just become acquainted with nylon stockings before the war, but now nylon was needed for parachutes, so to leg make-up (which rubbed off.)

The war was over in the Pacific in August 1945. After President Truman OK'd the dropping of atom bombs on Hiroshima and Nagasaki, Japan surrendered.

On April 12, 1945, my mother and I were shopping when we heard a newsboy call: "Extra, extra, read all about it - President Roosevelt is dead". We couldn't believe it. Just two months earlier this very ill president had participated in the Yalta Conference with Churchill and Stalin. Many felt America had been sold short because of Roosevelt's promises to Stalin. The Russians were given East Germany, cutting Berlin in half. Russia agreed to enter the Pacific war within 3 months of the surrender of Germany.

Russia did enter the Pacific war as our ally, but only after the war was virtually over. The atom bomb had already been dropped! However, Stalin claimed North Korea (Communism in N. Korea would later lead to the Korean War).

The problems that followed the division of Germany were many. The Iron Curtain between East and West Germany denied the German people the privilege of traveling back and forth and tourism into East Germany was impossible. Much of this might have been avoided except for the decisions of a very sick president. West Berlin rebuilt quickly under the American occupation, but East Berlin, under Russia, kept its war-torn look for years.

General Eisenhower returned to a hero's welcome. He visited Kansas City, and I wanted very much to go over to the Liberty Memorial to see him but I was nine-months pregnant and decided against it, especially since George was out on the road and I would have to go alone on the streetcar.

On June 30, 1945, our son George Jeffrey was born. We were still making our home with my parents. Tony was a sweet, gentle little boy and Jeffrey was such a happy, good baby, that it made difficult days ahead a little easier.

Golda's health started to decline. The doctors had not returned from the war and she had difficulty finding adequate medical attention. She died at home in October, of complications caused by her diabetes. Aunt Sylvia had helped me care for her for several months.

George and I had bought a house, but could not leave my mother when she was so sick. After her death, we moved to our new home at 1027 Cleveland KCK, and asked my father to come live with us. Baby Jeffrey helped to fill his empty arms.

On June 13, 1948, Arthur had cataract surgery at K U Medical Center. This was quite an operation in those days. It required two weeks stay in the hospital at $10 a day. He had to lie on his back with sand bags at each side of his head to keep it immovable. Today cataract surgery is almost an out-patient treatment.

On June 16, 1948, Mark Packard Allen was born at St. Luke's Hospital. Tony had taken his big brother status seriously when Jeff was born, and was not sure he could handle two little brothers. Jeff found giving up the position of the baby in the family was a rather sobering experience. Baby Mark was unconcerned and grew up to be his own little self who did not need help, thank you.

Jeff and Tony by Cleveland house about 1948

Now with three adults and three sons, by George, we thought it was time to look for more space. We moved out into the county, to a very large old house with an acre of land at 3354 N. 60th Street. The house cost $10,500. When we moved there in 1949, the streets were not numbered. In telling someone how to find us, we had to say we lived on

Orchard Road, two blocks west of Brenner Heights Road and five blocks north of Leavenworth Road; we were really out in the boon docks.

There was a crank telephone on the wall and an eight-party line. There were few secrets in that neighborhood! Of course, listening was frowned upon, but it was surprising how much leaked out. If one were lucky enough to find the line available, he cranked the handle on the side of the telephone to get the operator. After giving her the desired number, she would ring it. As I remember, the ring which was ours to answer was two short and three long rings.

Our house had five bedrooms, a sleeping porch, a full attic and basement. There was a heavy stone foundation and stone railing across the large front porch. We foolishly put a baby gate across the opening of the porch railing, thinking we could confine our venturesome little two-year-old Mark. He soon discovered that he could scale the railing, hang on by his little fingertips and drop four or five feet down on the other side to freedom! Tony and Jeff gave up trying to catch him, all they could do was to report him missing.

There was plenty of play room on the front half acre, and plenty of garden space on the back half. We had a large strawberry patch and chicken house. Mark thought it was a lot of fun to let the chickens out of their pen so they could scratch in our fussy neighbor's garden. (This was the neighbor who would keep a ball that Tony or Jeff had allowed to go in her yard. She wanted neither boys, nor chickens around).

We were among the last in the neighborhood to buy a television set, but finally gave in to keep our boys at home, as "all" of their friends had TV. The 1935 Pontiac was still our mode of transportation. On hot nights, we could take a ride to cool off and stop for an ice cream cone. During lightning storms or on noisy fourth of Julys, our big cowardly collie dog, Paddy, could be found waiting in the car for us. We did allow her to go along, but the ice cream cones were not too safe.

Our friends from in town, the Whittier's, thought our life style looked pretty good, so they moved out into our neighborhood and we had fun together.

-1950s –

We now had news reported in newspapers, on the radio and television. We heard about American involvement in the Korean Conflict, of gasoline wars in which the price of gasoline dropped to nineteen cents a gallon, and of the progress in our space program. Of course, Russia launched the first satellite, Sputnik I (1957) However, American scientists soon allowed us to overcome the Russian lead.

Styles for the girls called for full circular skirts, held out by wearing five or six ruffled, starched petticoats. This presented a problem for the school busses, and the halls in schools were too narrow to accommodate such "wide" girls. Boys were wearing shear nylon shirts that required no ironing. Things were looking up for mamas who had to do the ironing. Another ten years would see polyesters come into vogue. This also required no ironing. It is such a pity that fads do not stay when they are as good as this, polyester is out now and anyone seen in it is considered old fashioned.

School bussing had started after the Supreme Court ruled that schools should be integrated. Black children in the inner city were bussed out to the county, and all-black schools were either closed, or made into magnet schools which would attract white students. I had some misgivings about taking students out of their neighborhood schools. As a switchboard operator at Washington High School, I had to take morning attendance calls and heard many times that students had missed the bus and had no way to get to school.

Our move to the big house proved to be a very happy one, and necessary as our family was to be increased once more. Thomas Scott was born on July 10, 1952. His mother and dad thought he was the cutest little guy ever, but his 3 big brothers could only say they were glad he was not a girl. That summer, Tony left for his first Boy Scout camp experience at

Camp Naish. Brother Jeff was involved in Cub Scouts and little league baseball, and brother Mark was busy becoming an independent little four-year-old. Life in the Allen household was pretty lively!

George and Ruth on Christmas 1947

Baby furniture was a problem as we had given all of our baby things to the flood relief, following the devastating flood of 1951 in Kansas City, Kansas. We had to start over furnishing a nursery. I was happy to have an automatic washing machine, even though it was in the basement which was two flights of stairs down. There was no drier yet, but I did have a permanent line which beat having to string up a rope between trees. We had a dishwasher which was well used with seven people eating meals.

Arthur's health was steadily declining. He had several heart attacks which left him feeble and confused. In order to get the care he needed, he was moved to Sharon Lane Nursing Home, where Aunt Sylvia had gone after her stroke. We lost them both in 1958.

In 1958, Tony graduated from high school and left immediately for Montana where he was to work as a lookout on Haystack Mountain. He was alone in his station and his only contact with the outside world was by way of a two-way radio. He called for groceries which were then brought half way up the mountain and hung in a tree, away from animals. His lookout was glassed on all four sides to allow for easy spotting of fires. These windows needed to be kept clean. His only source of water was down the mountain, so water usage was budgeted and recycled very carefully. After holding out drinking water, the rest was used for cooking, then for dishwashing, then window washing, and finally bathing , which for a teen- age boy on his own probably didn't have a high priority

Jeff, Mark, Ruth, George, Tom and Tony on vacation at Howard Lake, Minnesota resort about 1955

After buying a tent and lots of camping equipment, the family made a trip to Montana in August to pick up our big boy. We were shocked to find him with a beard! He looked good to us, but we were not the only ones he wanted to see. He drove back to Kansas, exceeding the speed limit, as he wanted to see his high school sweetheart, Gloria Miller.

Our camping trip was a happy experience and the first of many to be made to the west coast. We camped in most of the major National Parks. In Yellowstone, we watched the bears getting our garbage and in all of the parks we enjoyed the evening campfires when the ranger talked to us.

George had started his career as a Railway Mail Clerk in the Terminal in Kansas City, MO., but followed his brother, Edward's, example of working mail on the trains instead of in the terminal. On the last trip Edward was to take; he stepped off the train into the path of an oncoming car. Complications from this accident hospitalized him for eight months and crippled him for life. He never returned to the mail service, but did return to his first love, teaching. He was an excellent teacher and many young people gained from this tragic accident.

George's road schedule kept him away from home six out of nine days. His work gave us a regular income, but it was difficult to stretch it over all the needs of a growing family. We kept a teacher's baby for $10 a week, which helped a little. Later, I worked two evenings a week in the drug store. I gave the boys their haircuts (sometimes to their chagrin.) The haircuts then were crew cuts or flat tops, a carryover from the GI haircuts worn by the soldiers. I also cut Dad's and George's hair and thus saved twenty-five cents a head. Our garden gave us fresh vegetables with enough canned green beans and strawberry jam to last through the winter. Chickens provided enough eggs for us with a few extra to sell.

- 1960s -

Styles in the 60's allowed for the use of polyester, which required little care and packed so easily. Skirts were to go way above the knee when the miniskirts came in late in the decade. Of course fashion designers go to such extremes in order to keep us crazy women buying new clothes. No sooner had people gotten used to seeing women's legs all the way up (their modesty was protected by panty hose), when fashion decreed that the "Mini" look was out and the "Maxi" look was in - this dropped skirts down to the ankles!

Men's leisure suits were of polyester and could be washed and spun dry. It was great while it lasted, but they, too, had their day and were soon passé.

Everyone was wearing shorts for sportswear. The two-piece swim suit became more and more brief until the bikini was in vogue. Some of us poochie people do not look so good in bikinis.

Railway Mail was no more! Mail was no longer sent by train. Zip codes were added to mailing addresses. Such were changes in the post office as George returned to working as supervisor in the Kansas City, Kansas Post Office.

The tragic news of the assassination of President Kennedy was on November 22, 1963. That day, I was ironing and watching TV, when a bulletin was flashed on the screen that the President had been shot. TV coverage was complete and sadly sensational. The President had been campaigning in Dallas and was riding in an open convertible when he was shot. We watched and listened hour by hour, hoping to hear of his survival, but he was finally pronounced dead. Lyndon Johnson, Vice President, was sworn into the office of President on the plane returning to Washington DC from Dallas.

Space travel progressed from Alan Shepherd's first flight into space and John Glenn's orbiting the earth to Neil Armstrong's walking on the moon in 1967.

The Viet Nam situation had become very serious during Kennedy's administration. He had sent military advisors over. President Johnson escalated the war and troops were soon sent. Draft boards were again becoming active with more quotas to fill. Our involvement in Viet Nam was very unpopular among many of the young people who felt that this was a Civil War and we should stay out of it. Nevertheless, draft quotas were rising. Many young men fled to Canada to "dodge" the draft. A movement was started toward an anti-establishment life style in which young people defied convention. They lived in communes, let their hair grow long and got involved with drugs. They were know as "Hippies" and felt this was their only means of protesting fighting a war in which they did not believe.

Ruth with her daughters-in-law: Bride Janet (Tom), Ruth, Vicki(Mark), Susan (Jeff), Gloria (Tony)

Our Sons had to register on their 18th birthdays. Viet Nam was a full scale conflict (it was never declared a war) by the time Tom registered in 1970. Draft numbers had been drawn from a fish bowl and listed according to the order drawn. Jeff and Mark had numbers close to the top of the list, but Tom's was low enough that he could depend on being able to finish college without being called.

–1970s –

News of the '70s was of Richard Nixon and the Watergate Scandal, more space progress and the forming of O. P. E. C. [Organization of Petroleum Exporting Countries]

When President Nixon was campaigning for his second term, he and his staff were found guilty of bugging the democratic office in the Watergate Hotel. The press picked it up and would not let it go until there was a Congressional Hearing and Nixon resigned, the first president ever to do so. (The press had done the same thing when

Senator Ted Kennedy was involved in the Chappaquiddick scandal. All the publicity ruined Ted Kennedy's chances at the presidency). The press is powerful.

After Nixon's resignation, Gerald Ford followed him into office. Ford may have done some good things, but the only things I can remember about him was his ability to hit the gallery with his golf ball, and his ability to fall down steps.

Jimmy Carter was the next president. He was a graduate of Annapolis Naval Academy, and a peanut farmer. He was a devout man and one of integrity. However when he was in office, we had double-digit inflation and the unemployment was greatly increased. Airplanes were being hijacked and we were beginning to have trouble with Iran. There were 80 hostages captured in Iran and Carter tried every means available to get them freed while he was in office. They were held for over a year and not released until after Ronald Reagan took office. I always felt sorry for Carter that he could not have had this one last victory.

Ronald Reagan, an ex-movie star, surprised many people with his strong administration. He had a smooth, articulate way of dealing with people. While in office, he was nearly killed by an assassin and had several bouts with cancer.

O.P.E.C. was formed by the Oil Producing countries to regulate prices of oil. They regulated to such an extent that there was a real shortage. Filling stations often had no gasoline to sell and when they did get a little, lines of cars soon formed. Many waited for an hour to get a few gallons, hoping it would still be there when their turn came. There was a small limit allowed. Where gasoline prices during the gas wars in the '50s were nineteen cents, they now soared to $1.49. We considered $1.25 a gallon quite reasonable.

This gas shortage caused car companies to take a second look at their "gas guzzlers". People were already discovering the economy of small cars imported from Germany and Japan. The two countries we had defeated in the war and were now occupying were having a healthy economy, thanks to O.P.E.C. The strong unions in the United States had pushed prices of domestic cars way up, so the car companies felt a double whammy.

As a solution to being dependent on oil from Middle East, the United States started drilling for oil in the Gulf and tapped the supply in Alaska. The Alaskan pipe line was quite a production. It had to be raised high enough over the tundra so melting would not cause pipe fractures.

We are happy that there is an improvement in the gasoline shortage, as George and I have been going to Florida for the winter since 1978. We share a home with his sister, Louise and her husband, Glenn Rawlins, on Anna Marie Island. George and his sister have found a real joy in these reunions after having been separated by the death of their mother when they were children. Glenn is an avid golfer and introduced the game to us, for which we will be forever grateful. We have bicycles down there and enjoy a two mile ride to the library. These times with the Rawlins are so special.

The beach is only a few short blocks away and we enjoy walking on the white sand of the Gulf. In the evening, we watch spectacular sunsets and are entertained by the antics of the dolphins and pelicans. We have made some very dear friends on Anna Maria.

Another change in our lives happened in 1965 when we sold the big old house and built a ranch style brick house at 2511 N 82nd Terrace. We had lived in the old house for 15 years and our sons were a little perturbed that we would part with it. We have enjoyed living on a smaller scale, though. We now have a VCR for our television set. We enjoy going to garage sales and filling up the play room with toys for the grandchildren (and Grandma). We are now driving a 1985 Oldsmobile Ciera which was a front-wheel drive and a trunk big enough for sets of golf clubs. We miss the LTD, but they don't build them like that anymore.

Ruth made quilts for all of her Grandchildren: Here is the quilt she made for Brian when he was a teenager. Ruth with Brian and his partner Matt Smith.

-LOOKING BACK-

In these reflections, I see that the world has changed a great deal in my lifetime. We have gone through World War II, Korean Conflict, and Viet Nam. We have survived the great depression.

We have gone from having women being homemakers whose time was given entirely to domesticity to women sharing the work world with men. We have gone from a free enterprise form of government to a socialistic one with many controls. We have seen Social Security come into effect as a retirement subsidy in 1935, but today it is the sole retirement of many.

We have seen black people striving for equality with whites. I pray this may come soon, but there is still so much racial unrest, we have a long way to go.

We have seen a new morality rise in which marriage is not considered a binding contract and many young people do not think it is even necessary. Personally, I like the old fashioned way with its love, security, and stability.

We have seen such diseases as diphtheria, small pox, measles, and polio practically eliminated through vaccination. Polio was a real threat as I was growing up and even when our sons were small. In the summer, we would rest for a couple of hours through the heat of the day as a preventative measure. We still need a cure for cancer and for AIDS.

Finally, I have gone from a baby in Topeka to a great-grandmother in Kansas City. I thank the dear Lord for giving me the parents, husband, sons, daughters-in law, grandchildren, and great grandchildren He did.

So, Grandmother Packard, our story goes on through your son, Arthur and his bride, Golda. Each of the progenies has been truly blessed to have the heritage given to us by Georgiana and George Washington Packard. Thank you.

AFTERGLOW

It is now 1998 and I am copying my story on the computer. What happy memories this has brought of the times that George and I had together.

We stopped going to Florida in 1992 when we sold our house and moved to Lakeview Retirement Village. Louise and Glenn came to see us for George's birthday in August 1995. Louise had undergone cancer surgery and George was getting ready to go on dialysis. I'm sure they both felt this would be their last meeting in this world. George died in October and Louise died the next June. Glenn is in a Retirement Center in Florida and we still stay in touch.

Our sons, daughters-in-law, grandchildren, and great grandchildren are the most special people on this earth and are my constant joy and comfort. I am so blessed and pray that each member of the family may look back on his or her life some day and have the same feeling of fulfillment I have today.

George and Ruth Allen 50th Wedding Anniversary Photo

7 ADDENDUM II

Ruth Packard Allen Photos

Ruth Elizabeth Packard's Great Grandmothers

Elizabeth Webster Packard, Mother of both Cyrus Packard and Lewis Packard. Also the cousin of Daniel Webster

Sarah Anderson Barr on the left and her sister Tamza. Sarah was the Mother of John Barr, Grandmother of Florella Stafford Barr, and Great Grandmother to Ruth Elizabeth Packard.

Grandparents of Ruth Elizabeth Packard

George Washington Packard with Grandson Stafford Packard about 1912

George Washington and Georgiana Packard

Florella Stafford Barr, mother of Golda

John Barr sitting in a railroad caboose. He died in 1910 so the photo was earlier than that.

Ruth Packard's parents

Child Golda Barr, at left with her Mother Florella and a studio photo on the right. Note the boardwalk sidewalk.

Golda Barr 3rd from the left on a Pommel Horse at a YWCA Gym Show

Tony Allen

Golda Barr at 16

Arthur Packard as a young man

Young Ruth Packard

John Bishop with impish Ruth on the right, Ruth with doll, Buddy Lee and on the bottom Ruth with her cat Puff.

On a family outing at a park: Arthur, Charles, Golda, Gene, Ruth and Stafford

A favorite outing was to walk to the Quindaro Ruins where Cyrus and Georgiana Packard landed in 1857. On the left: Ruth, Gene, Golda, with Arthur standing in the middle and Charles on the right. Note even on outings the boys and Arthur wore ties and Arthur a coat while Golda and Ruth wore dresses and hats.

Studio photo with Stafford in back, Golda, Gene, Ruth in front, Arthur and Charles

Ruth's brothers, Stafford, Gene and Charles in the early 1920s and Gene, Charles in his Navy uniform and Stafford after his stroke in 1943.

Arthur and Golda in about 1944 in their home at 724 32nd Street, Kansas City, Kansas

Arthur at work

My Common, Remarkable Family

At a Packard family reunion: Charles and Helen Packard, George and Ruth Allen and Ruth and Gene Packard

Charles, Ruth and Gene at the reunion

Allen Family Reunion at Holiday Island on Table Rock Lake, Arkansas in August of 1995. From Left back row; Jeff his wife Susan, Gloria, (our oldest son Paul and his wife Janet's oldest daughter) Challis, Tony, Paul and Janet's 2nd Daniel Bradley, Paul and Janet's 3rd Austin, Ruth, George, Paul, Janet holding their 4th Taylor, Mark, Janet (Tom's wife Janet), Vicki, and Brian (Tom and Janet's eldest); in front Katie (Mark and Vicki's 3rd), Tim (Tom and Janet's youngest), Lindsay (Mark and Vicki's) and Tom. This picture was taken about 2 months before George died.

Gail Geiger, Mary and Gus Geiger's daughter, Ruth Allen and Tony Allen

My Common, Remarkable Family

Family celebration remembering George Allen's 100th birthday. Back Row: Tom Allen, Jeff Allen, Susan Allen, Glenn Robinson (friend of Ruth Allen), Gloria Allen, Mark Allen, Vicki Allen, Scott Simon (friend of Lindsay and a year later her husband), Lindsay, Katie Whitehead and husband Gabe Whitehead; Front Row: Tony Allen, Janet Allen, Ruth Allen, Mandy Allen, Elliot Allen, Tim Allen

Ruth Allen with Great Granddaughter and namesake Lena Ruth Allen

(daughter of Joel and Jil Allen and Granddaughter of Jeff and Susan)

Ruth Allen in her apartment at Lakeview Retirement Village where she and George moved in 1992. Photo by her Grandson Paul Allen in 2011.

8 THIS IS ME BY GEORGE

George Hadley Allen

As told to his wife Ruth about 1994

Preface

For years Mom tried to get Dad to write some of his childhood stories. It was always something he was going to do in the future, but never seemed to get around to it. In 1994 when Dad was ill and they had time on their hands, Mom came up with a solution. She talked to Dad about his Childhood, growing up and their time together and would type the stories. She and Dad would then go over them and Dad would decide on any changes. So thanks to Mom we have preserved some of Dad's childhood memories. Of course it is presented as Mom wrote it and I suspect that many of the stories after Mom and Dad got married represent Mom's memory as well as Dad's.

The last couple of pages of Dad's story were added in 1995 after they made their last trip to the West to meet new great grandchildren. Our trip to Maui was a treasure for all of us as was the Allen family reunion on Table Rock Lake in August of 1995. Dad died in October of that year.

The final letter I transcribed was a letter Dad wrote to his cousin Alice and he referenced another cousin Julia, her sister Mary and an Uncle Claude. Claude was the husband of Sarah Nevada (Vada) Dunlap and Julia and Mary their daughters. I believe Alice was the daughter of Earnest Charles Dunlap. I have a copy of the letter and I made minor changes to correct spelling and grammar, but tried not to change any of the content or meaning. This letter obviously served as the source Mom and Dad used for several of the early stories.

Tony Allen

This is Me by George

HARMON ALLEN

Much of what I am writing was told to me as stories by my father, Harmon Allen. He was a great story teller.

Harmon was born near French Lick, Indiana. It was called French Lick because the area had a lot of salt above the ground where the animals came to lick the rocks of salt. Also, there was a spring in the area where the water was a very strong physic. It was bottled as Pluto Water and sold all over the country.

Harmon's father was Levi Allen and his mother was Jane Seybold Allen. Their children were: Harmon, Amanda, Minnie, Thomas, May, and Elsie. The Allen and Seybold families did not believe in having more than one name.

Levi's parents were Jeremiah and Leah Hobson Allen. Leah's parents came from Ireland so there's "something in me Irish". I want to tell you about my grandmother, Jane Seybold. She was quite a lady.

The name, Seybold, according to legend comes from a small boat named the Sea Bowl. The Sea Bowl boat was common in Holland and

Germany. Once a little baby boy was found in a Sea Bowl. The people who found him, kept him. They could not find his parents and he had no name, so they called him the Sea Bowl baby. Over the years the name Sea Bowl became Seybold.

BAck row: Left to right - Elsie, Minnie, Harmon, Mae, and Amanda
Front row: Levi and Jane Seybold Allen

Harmon was George's Father

My great grandfather, Thomas Seybold, was a miller. He had a water-powered mill where the farmers came to have their grain ground. The miller kept a percentage of the grain for his fee. Thomas Seybold also had a brewery as most millers did in those days. The end product was whiskey. His daughter, Jane (my grandmother) made the best whiskey around. She even had whiskey named for her, Jane's Whiskey. She hated it because her father and two brothers were alcoholics.

Grandma Jane had a broken knee and she had no doctor to set it. As a consequence, she limped. She told me that she broke her leg when she was picking cherries and fell out of the tree. She made good dried apples which they ate for dessert. One time Grandpa caught a coon, which he cooked and was anxious to eat. He took a bite of coon, and then reached for a bite of apple. Pretty soon it was a bite of coon and many bites of apple. Finally he pushed the coon aside and said: "Coon will be coon!"

Once on a vacation, Ruth and I stopped in Paoli, Indiana, and met a second cousin, Paul Waynick, who took us around the area where my grandparents had lived. Most of the farm including their house had been covered by a lake that was formed when a dam was built. This cousin also took us to the church where Grandpa and Grandma were members. Miles Allen, their oldest son, is buried in the church graveyard.

My father's first memory of a home in Indiana was of a small log cabin. The side of the cabin is where the fireplace was to be was not completed when winter set in, so they piled logs up in front of the empty space where there was no fireplace and built a huge fire. This served for heating and cooking. (Of course this was outside the cabin). Every spring, the farmers in the area would tap the sugar maple trees for the sap. They would bring the sap and cook it in huge cast iron pots. It was boiled down to thick syrup. Very little of the Syrup was boiled down to Sugar. Syrup was about the only sweetener the farmers had. The "boil down", was a big family event. They had square dances, bag races, horse shoe pitching, and much gossip. In those days the farms were far from town. Newspapers were rare and most were old by the time the people got them; so much of the news was passed on at public gatherings like the "boil down."

My grandfather and grandmother decided to come to Kansas about 1878 with neighbors who were coming to Kansas for free land. They travelled by covered wagon and took only their cooking utensils, a barrel of water, a cow for milk, and the clothes they were wearing. My father was about seven years old. Aunt Elsie was the only one born in Kansas. On the trip, their young son, Thomas died.

They homesteaded in LeLoup, Kansas on 40 acres which was used to raise food for eating the next year. Most of the bread they ate was cornbread and the only sweetener was black strap molasses. They raised their own meat, mostly chickens and hogs.

My grandfather did a lot of hunting in those days, not for fun but for meat. He mainly was a farmer, but in the late fall and winter he worked on the section gang of the Santa Fe Railroad. In those days they were building the Atchison, Topeka, and Santa Fe. Grandpa Levi died about 1918 and Grandma Jane died in 1926, the same year that my mother died, so Harmon lost his dear mother and dear wife the same Year.

In Kansas, Harmon grew up in a very religious family. On Sunday, when everyone else was resting (you didn't work on Sunday), Harmon slipped out and went hunting for rattlesnakes with his little yellow dog.

Harmon attended a little country school and then Baker University where he prepared for the ministry. He knew Bishop Quail (the grandfather of Dan Quail). He taught school in the Indian Territory in Oklahoma before Oklahoma was a state. He had both white and Indian boys who did not get along well. One day, a white boy brought a gun to school and an Indian boy had a hunting knife. Daddy took the gun and knife and gave the boys a spanking. The next day a large Indian buck appeared and asked Daddy if he had spanked his son. Daddy said, "Yes." The Indian smiled, held out his hand and said, "I want to shake the hand of the man who could spank my son."

Harmon left teaching to go into the pulpit. While serving as a minister in the Methodist Church in Howard, Kansas, he met Mary Dunlap. They fell in love and were married.

MARY DUNLAP

This would be a good time to tell you about my mother and her family. Mary Elizabeth Dunlap was a daughter of Joseph Alexander Dunlap and Harriett Samantha Billingsley. A family legend tells of "our ancestor," King George III.

Grandpa's father was Alexander Dunlap who married Mary Rex. She was a descendent of George Rex who was born in England and was the son of King George III by a commoner wife. After the king ascended to the throne, the marriage was dissolved and the wife and son were sent to America. As long as he lived, George Rex received an income from England, so who knows!

Now, back to Grandpa Joseph. His schooling had consisted of three months each year until he was 14 years old. At that time, he began working in the coal mines. He was a coal miner until he moved from California, PA to Kansas at age 25. He was a great reader and had an outstanding memory. A copy of his will is in this book.

Harriett Billingsley was born in California, PA. She was the daughter of a wealthy man, Moses Billingsley, who made his fortune by building rafts and loading them with coal. He floated the coal down the Ohio and Mississippi Rivers and sold coal along the way. He sometimes got as far as New Orleans before all his coal was gone. He then sold the raft for wood and returned home by steamboat, where he started all over with another raft.

Harriett's five brothers served in the Civil War. Harry, the youngest died of starvation in the Andersonville Prison. Joseph and Harriett were parents of 8 children. When they moved to Kansas, they had three little girls, my mother was the oldest. The rest of the children were born in Kansas.

Harriett was a conscientious mother, knitting wool stockings for her family and making quilted petticoats for her daughters for the winter. She had a strong, clear voice that carried across the prairie.

She suffered from homesickness and it was 13 years before she was able to go back to Pennsylvania to visit her family. She had consented to move to Kansas because of the great danger of Joseph's work in the coal mines.

Dunlap Family: Back row; Anna Dunlap (Harrison), Emma Mae Dunlap, James Harrison Dunlap, Mary Elizabeth Dunlap (Allen), Sarah Nevada Dunlap (Taylor) Front Row; Jim Norwell Dunlap, Mother Harriett Samantha Billingsly Dunlap, Joseph A. Dunlap and Ernest Charles Dunlap

Since the first three children were girls, Mary Elizabeth, the oldest, had to be her father's helper on the farm. She went to Bunker Hill School, walking one and a half miles across the prairie. At the age of 16, she decided that in some way she was going to have an education. She enrolled at Kansas State Normal, now Emporia State University. The first year she had no money and worked as a housekeeper for her board and room. This was too much so she took a year off to teach to get enough money for another year of college. So by alternating teaching a year and going to college a year, she was able to finish her education. She also helped her younger sisters and brothers to get theirs. She bought some calves for her father and years later, when he sold them, he sent the money to her.

Mary was teaching when she met the handsome, red-haired preacher, Harmon Allen and so the story continues.

GEORGE ALLEN IS BORN

When Mary and Harmon married, they planned to go to Northwestern University where each could pursue further education. However, Mary soon discovered that she was to be a mother, so her education was put on hold.

While at Northwestern, Harmon had a Public Speaking class under Professor Comnock, a Scotchman from Edinburgh University. Harmon was an apt pupil and with the fine training he received in this class, he became a popular public speaker and his congregations profited from his unique talent. He had the Scotch dialect down pat. He was a born actor and taught his children to love Shakespeare's plays by reading and acting them out. His son, Edward, had the same gift. As my big brother, Edward used to read Shakespeare to me and we would pretend that he was Sir Andrew Augercheck and I was Sir Toby Belch.

When Harmon and Mary left Northwestern to take a pastorate at Mound City, Ks., they had two children, Joseph and Harriett. Edward was born in Mound City. His next church was in Cherokee where Mary was born. Then on to Caney where I was born.

Caney was near the Oklahoma border and a group of Elks and Eagles were having a convention. Kansas was a dry state, but they arranged for the liquor for their convention to be stored in a train car on the Oklahoma side of the border. Daddy was violently opposed to drinking, so with the help of some W.C.T.U. (Women's Christian Temperance Union) Ladies, he went to the train car and broke every bottle of whiskey. The convention was spoiled and my father's name was MUD! He was rocking me in front of the window one day and a brick was thrown through the window. It just missed my head. Daddy could have been lynched, tarred and feathered, or who knows what, when he went into town soon after the whiskey incident. He was grabbed by several angry men. A little man, sitting on the curb, saved the day. He started laughing. One of the men asked why he was laughing, He said, "This is the first time I ever saw a little red-headed woodpecker drive 500 Elks and Eagles out of town!" Tension was relaxed and my father was released.

However, his stand against drinking made him unpopular with the church where the chairman of the official board owned a saloon. They virtually starved him out. He was getting $10 a month and had a family of 5 children to feed. When my mother heard of the job opening at Lansing State Prison where the Chaplain's pay was $140 a month, she started packing.

I was one year old when we moved to Lansing. When I was old enough to ride my tricycle, I often rode it as I accompanied Daddy to the prison to say grace. When people asked me what I wanted to be when I grew up, I would say "A Prisoner." It was at Lansing that my little sister, Elizabeth Louise was born. I remember the night. Mary and Harriett were taking care of me and told me that if I made a noise, the boogie man would get me and I believed them!

While at Lansing, we spent summers on the farm at Edison Station where the children picked berries and were paid at the end of the summer with a calf. Joseph started his herd this way. Joseph started his college at Park College. While there, he enlisted in the Army. However, he was not in the Army long before the Armistice was signed and World War I was over. I remember watching the returning soldiers and bands marching down the streets of Leavenworth. Joseph did not have to see action and was able to resume his college education. He finished his degree at Kansas State University at Manhattan.

Harmon and family moved to Leavenworth in 1918. He was now the chaplain at the Federal Penitentiary. One of his first jobs was to tour the United States to investigate conditions of Federal Prisons. Since Daddy was to be away so much, Mama decided to move to Manhattan to keep house for Joseph. She packed up her brood, which now consisted of Harriett, Edward, Mary, George and baby Louise.

I was in the second grade. Harriett was a senior in high school and was able to take some music courses at the university. The following year we returned to Leavenworth and Joseph and Harriett stayed in Manhattan to pursue their degrees.

Young George and his little sister Louise

Daddy always made breakfast for the children, biscuits, red-eye gravy (ham gravy) and coffee soaks. His biscuits were large. He put half of a biscuit in a mug, buttered it, poured coffee over it and then put on the other half. He added sugar and more coffee and cream. That was his famous coffee soak!

My childhood at Leavenworth was a happy one. I had for pets a pony, a nanny goat, rabbits, pigeons, and a big dog named Shep, who took care of me.

Leavenworth was a high-type prison. Among the prisoners were many professional men including doctors, lawyers, teachers, etc. Daddy's secretary was a bank president who had been caught embezzling funds. Also any Indian who committed a crime on the reservation was sent to Leavenworth.

Back Row: Mary Francis, Edward, Harriet, Joseph, Front Row: Harmon (father), Louise, Mary (mother), George

As chaplain, Daddy was entitled to have prisoners to help around the house and yard. My mother didn't approve of having them around us, but she did agree to one Yard man.

George Allen as a Boy Scout

The first one we had was Archibald Jones, or Midnight, as he was called. He was just as black as his name implies. With six children in the family, Mama was pretty busy and so Midnight gradually began to ride herd on me. I loved that man, and although Midnight was a crook, he was always a gentleman around the family. He was finally released on parole.

Daddy vas very much involved with the Indians. One of the things he did, with the help of the Indians, was to have a Powwow every Fourth of July. One of the decorations they had was a full sized Indian Tepee. That is how I first met Ben Long Ear. Ben was the son of the fourth wife of the head Chief of the Crow Indian Tribe. As the son of a chief, he was raised much like a prince. Ben was a tall man, about six feet tall, straight as an arrow, and a proud man. He could read and write and was a very good artist. He was excellent at handling animals of any kind.

When Midnight was paroled, Ben was the next yard man. By that time, I was about nine years old. I said Ben was good at handling animals; he was equally good at handling a lively nine-year-old boy. Being with Ben was a learning experience. He taught me a lot of things that he would have taught a son of his own.

Ben was a very good story teller. He told me a lot of old Crow legends. When he told a story, he would get down on his haunches, take a stick and draw a map or illustrate his story. He told of the Crow Tribe's favorite animal, the fox. I won't say that the fox was a God, but he did some superhuman things and was very smart.

I always loved animals, but Ben taught me a lot about them. One time, he found two squabs. He brought them home and showed me how to soak corn and hand feed them by putting the corn in their beaks and stroking their throats to make the corn go down. Mine was a white squab and I named him McAdoo (McAdoo was the name of the democratic candidate for Vice President that year). Ben's was a blue squab who was named for the Presidential candidate, Al Smith.

One day I scratched my wrist when I was with Ben. He said he was going to make me a blood brother. He scratched his wrist until it bled. We put the two wrists together and the blood mingled and I was a blood brother of Ben's. He gave me the Indian name of Nutaba Cha Cher, which means in the Crow language, White Bear. So I guess I am a Crow Indian!

The whole family loved Ben. Mary couldn't believe that Ben had ever done anything bad, so she asked him why he was in prison. He said, "Because I killed a man." That is all he ever said about it. However, Daddy got a more detailed account of the crime at the prison.

Ben and his brother-in-law, who was a white man, took the family wagon to town one Saturday and got roaring drunk. On the way home, the brother-in-law started to tease Ben. They got into a fight and Ben had a knife.

When I was 10 years old, I started driving Joseph's Model-T Ford. He had rented a farm about four miles out of town on which to pasture his herd. Often he wanted some things from town and would send me in the truck. Mama was deathly afraid of Cars and she insisted that Ben go with me when I drove. This is funny because Ben knew nothing about cars. (Also, he was not supposed to be off the prison property.)

One day when Ben and I were at the farm, we heard Mrs. Hagg screaming for help. (Joseph rented the farm from the Haggs). To go back in time, there had been a fire in the Hagg's house and a lot of treasured keep-sakes were lost. Mrs. Hagg's daughter, Mrs. McDonald couldn't accept the loss and was in a deep depression. When Ben and I heard the screaming, it seemed to come from the barn, so we headed there.

We found Mrs. Hagg, a little old woman, holding her daughter around her knees. Mrs. McDonald was a big woman and had committed suicide by jumping out of the hay loft with a rope around her neck. Ben was up the ladder like a Cat and untied the rope and had Mrs. McDonald down, but it was too late. By that time Joseph showed up and I was sent packing. The County sheriff had to be called. Joseph knew the sheriff and asked him to leave Ben's name out of the report as he could be in trouble for being off the prison property. The sheriff agreed.

Ben had a lawyer working on his case trying to get him a parole. He was a full-blooded Indian by the name of Yellow Tail. Ben finally got his parole. The only time I ever saw him excited was when he came to tell us that the parole had come through. When he left to go back to Helena,

Montana we never saw or heard from him again. Edward and Willardean went to Helena in the 1960's to see if they could find out anything about him. Edward talked to one of his relatives and was told that Ben was dead. After he returned to the reservation he had been a chief in the tribal council and had served in that capacity until he died.

We had a large garden in Leavenworth and Mama was a good gardener. She canned much of our fruit and vegetables for the winter. She even preserved pork chops. She had a big milk churn in which she poured melted lard, then a layer of pork chops and another layer of lard. By alternating these two layers, she filled the churn. They kept well and were so good! I also remember using the churn for making butter. I was just a little guy and had to stand on a chair to be high enough to work the churn. I had a huge apron tied around my middle and really churned up a storm.

Mama loved animals, but her enthusiasm for cows was not shared by our papa. He said that if someone gave him the best cow in the world, he would be just as good as they were and give it right back.

While my mother was the disciplinarian of our family, she was also very loving. She was never too busy to take me on her lap. She always tucked me in bed at night and read to me. I remember her reading the book of Proverbs. She did not believe in reading fiction, especially the Westerns that I liked, but I managed to read them anyway. She was adamant about not using slang. She said that if it could not be said in good English, it did not need to be said at all. One of her expressions, when she was serious, was, "That's the word with the bark on it".

Mama was strong in her convictions, and one of them was kindness to children and animals. One day she looked across the street and saw a big bruiser of a man whipping his son with a buggy whip. My mother stormed over, grabbed the whip and took after him with it, saying, "Don't ever let me see you doing that again!" And he didn't!

It was truly a sad day when my mother went to the doctor and the family was told to take her home and make her comfortable. She had cancer, but the doctor did not say so. Mary dropped out of Baker University to help care for her mother. Louise and I were kept away from Mama. I think it was because she could not bear to see us and know that, she could not raise us.

After my mother died in 1926, my life was changed forever. The next few years are almost too painful for me to remember so I'll skip through them briefly. Daddy gave up the prison work. I was in Lawrence during my Jr. High School years. Mary, Edward, and I rented an apartment over a drug store.

Mary and Edward were students at K.U. and I was in Jr. High. I was separated from my little sister, Louise, for the first time, and I did not know how much I would miss her.

Lawrence Junior High School 1928 Basketball team while George was living with the Harnar family. George is back row right next to the coach.

In my sophomore year of high school, I was without a home until Edward took me to the Harnar home. Edward was engaged to Willardean Harnar. Mrs. Harnar, Willardean's mother, made me feel welcome as she took me in and gave me a room. Edward stayed with me the first night. What a brother! Mrs. Harnar was a real friend. I also had two school friends in Lawrence whose mothers kind of adopted me. What would I have done without supportive sisters, brothers, and friends!

George Allen with cast in Ottawa High School Jr. Play, George on the far left.

Joseph helped me with expenses at KU the first two years. In exchange, I worked summers for him in the dairy. The 3rd year was my last one at KU. I had finished my pre-med courses, but without more backing medicine was out of the question as a career. Joseph rented a place in Leavenworth and Edward and Willardean ran a water business. I drove Joseph's truck down into Missouri to get spring water, which I bottled and took back to Leavenworth to sell at the Fort. Edward was teaching school in Cheney, Ks. and was unable to be with us a lot. Willardean ran the business and took care of their two children, T.K. and Phyllis. When Edward came home for the summer, he took over my job and I was unemployed.

RUTH PACKARD ON THE SCENE

Mary asked me to come to Kansas City to try to find a job. She let me stay with her and her husband, Gus Geiger. This was in the summer of 1935 when jobs were almost nonexistent, toward the end of the great depression. I was lucky enough to get a job in the milk department of the Borden Milk Co.

Mary was a member of the Western Highlands Presbyterian Church. She told me about the active young people's group (Christian Endeavor), which was sponsored by Mary and Stafford Packard. Mary Packard had been my sister Mary's kitchen mate in Watkins Hall at K.U. I was not surprised when I was invited to a picnic the group was having in Stafford and Mary's back yard. I knew none of the young people, but meeting people was easy for me. There was quite a crowd of people my age. After we were served hot dogs and a cold drink, I noticed across the yard from me, the prettiest little brunette that I had ever seen. She wore a cute little brown outfit and had the cutest little feet!

She was wearing little brown walking shoes, I still remember them. The combination was striking. I soon found out that her name was Ruth Packard and that she was the sister of Stafford. She was shy, but I was interested.

However, it was several months before we actually went out together and even then it was not of our own doing. Our minister, Dr. Claggett, asked if I would go to a church banquet with him and his wife. They picked me up and I was surprised when they headed for Ruth's house. It seems they had also invited Ruth without telling her that I would be along. Neither of us minded. We had a good time and that was the beginning of our dating.

I did not have a car, so dating was done by streetcar or walking to church or to the drug store to buy coffee, sodas, or just sitting on the front porch swing "talking."

While living in college towns, I had the opportunity of attending plays and learned to love the legitimate theater. It was fun introducing this form of art to Ruth. We saw such plays as "Victoria Regina" with Helen Hayes and "Arsenic and Old Lace" with Boris Karloff. Also we saw George M. Cohan in "I'd Rather be Right" We went to the KC Blues games (a farm team of the Yankees), and I made a baseball fan of my girl. We had four years of fun while Ruth went to Jr. College for two years and Business College for another two years. On Sunday, we usually went to the Pla-Mor Ballroom and danced to big bands. Often we double dated with Ruth's cousin, Dale Bishop, and his girlfriend, Altheda Berkey. After the dance, we went to the Christian Endeavor meeting.

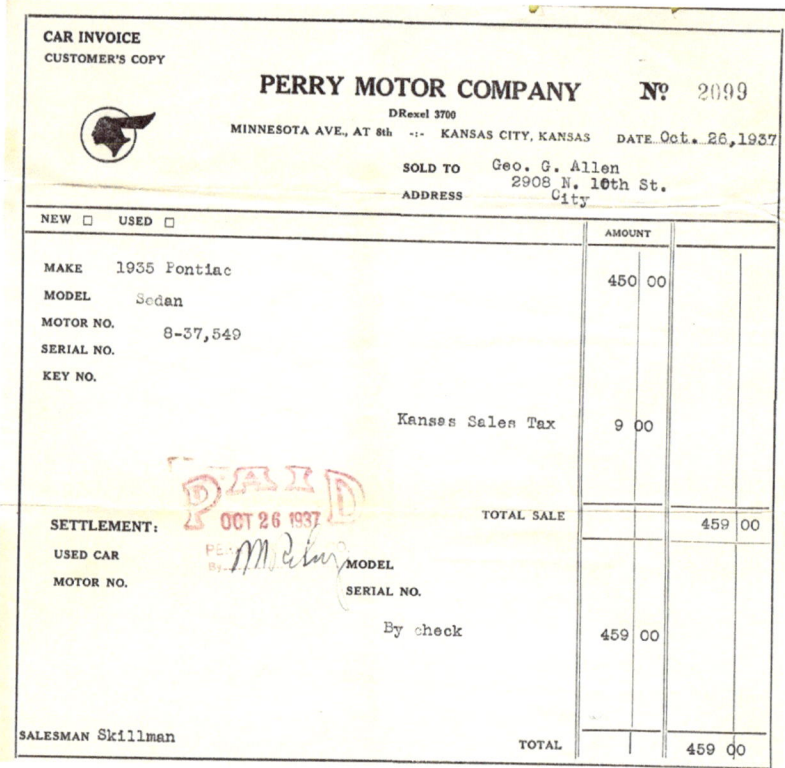

Invoice for 1935 Pontiac George bought so he could date Ruth

The Packard's bought a house many miles away so I had to buy a car, or find a new girlfriend that lived closer. I opted for the car. In 1937 I bought a 1935 Pontiac, which served us well for many years.

Gus told me of a Civil Service Examination, which was to be given. In 1935, I took the examination for Clerk/Carrier in the Post Office. I passed with a good grade and was called for an interview with the postmaster. The interview was for 8:00 a.m. There was to be an examination for

Railway Mail Service at 9:00 a.m. I figured I could take it after the interview. The postmaster did not show up, so I left to take the other exam, which I also passed. When I saw the postmaster, he asked why I had failed to keep my appointment. I told him that, since he was not there and I needed a job, I took the R.M.S. Exam." He said the reason for the interview was to tell me that I had a job in the Post Office if I wanted it. I started working as a substitute carrier, but did not get much work. When I was notified that I could have an appointment in the Railway Mail Service, I took it, and have never been sorry. Edward had taken the examination when I did, so we both ended up running on mail trains.

George and Ruth while dating and Studio photo George gave Ruth while they were dating

One time Edward stepped out of the mail car at a station to get some food, and was hit by a car. He was in the hospital for eight months and was permanently crippled. He was unable to return to working mail and went back to his first love, teaching. He was a really great teacher and influenced many young lives, including those of my sons.

My train years were filled with a camaraderie that I had never known before, and my friends from those years are still special to me. My first train was the Rock Island Rocket, a steam train which made a daily turn-around trip to Caldwell, Ks. After a few weeks, there was reorganization and I was put on a night run to Caldwell. It, too, was a turnaround run and I came home the next day. Later, they started running through Caldwell to Ft. Worth. I ran on a "Bud" car, which had been a commuter train. It was a single car with the 30 foot mail section in front and a passenger section behind. It had a gasoline- powered diesel engine, which turned both the front and back wheels and was run by a motorman.

We had a pretty nice arrangement with the Chef in the diner. For $1.00 we could get a full meal and all the coffee we could drink.

They took the Bud car off by the time I was a foreman, and I had to find another job. I chose the KC & Pueblo and ran two years on the Missouri Pacific to Pueblo. When Mo Pac trains no longer carried passengers and mail, I again changed jobs. This time it was to Chicago on the Ft. Mad. I thought if any train would not be taken off, it would be the Ft. Mad. Within a year, it happened. I was now really without a job as the Railway Mail Service was no more. I applied at the Kansas City, Kansas Post office and was hired as a supervisor. This is where I worked until I retired in 1975. While I was there, Mark got out of the Air Force and started working for the post office. He and I worked at the same Post office from 1972 until 1975.

To back up a few years, I was working in the Post office as a substitute carrier when Ruth and I were dating. I suggested several times that we should get married, but she wanted to finish her education. She surprised me in 1939 when I proposed, kind of out of habit, and she accepted! She even suggested that we get married and go to the World's Fair in New York with Dale and Altheda Bishop. Going on a honeymoon with another couple did not appeal to me, so I set the date of Feb.2, 1940. Being a sentimental guy, I felt, this date was special as it was 4 years to the day since I first kissed her. Also, it would help me to remember our anniversary as February 2 is Ground Hog's Day.

I was the last of my family to marry. Joseph had married Agneta Ellis, and they had 3 children: Joseph Ellis, George Rex and Virginia. Harriett had married Forrest Noll and they had 2 sons: Lewis Harmon and Forrest Lee. Edward had married Willardean Harnar and they had 2 children: T. Kramer and Phyllis Joan. Mary had married Gustav Geiger and they were parents of Gail Louise in 1941. Louise married Glenn Rawlins in 1937, and they have been close to all these nieces and nephews.

Ruth Packard and George Allen wedding party, Feb. 2, 1940

ENTER THE BOYS

We followed my parent's example of getting married in February and having a baby son on December 2nd of the same year. Charles Anthony (Tony) was a miracle to us. Of course, the miracle was the fact that he survived having such amateur parents. We filled many books with pictures of him. Four years later, when his brother, George Jeffrey (Jeff) was born, the country was at war and there was no film to be had, so there are few pictures of baby Jeff.

In 1942, Stafford had a stroke and he and Mary asked if we would take over the lease of their house as they wanted to move in with her parents. We were happy to do this. It was just up the street from Edward and Willardean. Little Tony used to come home from Edward's and let Tony's Mom find surprises in his pockets which Uncle Edward had put there, such neat things as worms or snails. These were happy times, but the landlady wanted her house back and would not renew the lease. During these war years, rents were frozen and landlords could afford to be selective, no pets or children. After a lot of frustrating unsuccessful searching for a place to rent, we appreciated the offer of the Packard's to share their home until we could find something. Tony was 3 years old when we moved and was happy to be with his grandparents.

The year 1945 was a happy one and a sad one. Jeffrey was born on June 30th, and his Grandma Packard died on Oct. 6th. The war was over and the soldiers were coming home. The days of rationing food, tires, and gasoline were over. President Roosevelt, the only president to be elected to 4 terms, died. It was an eventful year.

Arthur, Golda, Ruth, George, Tony in front

We had bought a house at 1027 Cleveland, KCK, but could not move as long as Ruth's mother needed her. I was running to Caldwell and was gone a lot, but not as much as if I had been in the service. I registered for the draft when we were first married, but my number did not come up until 1944. I went to Leavenworth for my physical, which I passed. They had no openings in the Navy (the service of my choice), so they told me to go home and wait until they contacted me. The war was over and I never heard from them.

After Grandma's death, we asked Grandpa Packard to remain part of our family and move with us. He lived with us for thirteen years. Some of the events which occurred while we were living on Cleveland, were: Aunt Sylvia Bishop's house burned across the street from us. She, Uncle Aaron and his mother moved in with us temporarily; Tony started school and had 3 years at Hawthorn Grade School; Baby Jeff had pneumonia and was hospitalized for 2 weeks; and another little son was added to our family. Mark Packard was a beautiful baby and did not take up much room, but we suddenly realized that we needed more space, so we bought our second house way out in Wyandotte County on Orchard Road. We later got a real address: 3354 N. 60th St. The house was a large, 10 room house on an acre of ground. It had a full attic and walk-out basement. It is a good thing we got a big house as we were again to be blessed with another beautiful son. Thomas Scott was born in 1952. I was indeed, a rich man with 4 sons. Little did I know how much they would enrich my life!

We moved to the county in 1949 and lived there 15 years. When we moved, Tony was in the 4th grade. When we left, he was at Oregon State working toward his PhD. When we moved, Jeff was 3 years old and when we left, he was a student at KU. Mark was only 1 year old when we moved, and he lived in that house until he was a junior in high school. Tom was born there and was in the 8th grade when we left. So it is understandable that the boys considered this their home and resented our selling it.

These 15 years were pretty frantic what with raising 4 active boys, having an ailing grandpa (he died in 1958), and running on the mail trains. The big old house needed constant repair and the half acre of garden was a big job. However, as I look back on these years, I do not seem to remember the frustrations as much as the happy times we had. We always had a big Christmas. Birthdays were special. The camping trips were unforgettable.

When Tony graduated from high school, he took a summer job working in the forest in Montana as a lookout. We wanted to drive back to get him at the end of the summer, but the only way we could afford to make the trip was by camping. So we bought a tent, sleeping bags, and set out. This was to be the first of many memorable trips as we camped in the National Parks throughout the country. The campfires in the evenings were educational and fun. The fire-fall at Yosemite was breath taking! They pushed the campfire over the mountain at the end of the evening and the fire falling was a real sight. They don't do that anymore.

For years we had just one car, usually a Ford. However, that changed in 1963 when we had an accident and Ruth broke the windshield of our Nash Rambler. We were on our way to Minnesota, but this stopped us in Iowa as the car was totaled. We flew home in the undertaker's little plane. When the insurance paid us, we had enough for a new car and an old car. We needed the extra as we soon had more drivers than cars!

I could write a book about each of our special sons, their special wives, special children, and special grandchildren. (Don't get me started bragging about my grandchildren, time and space do not allow.) I will try to summarize briefly their years with us.

Tony was a quiet, serious guy. He was active in scouting for years and helped many boys along the way. He went to Ottawa University and in his senior year, he had his beautiful bride with him. He had dated Gloria Miller since they met at a scout picnic years before. They went to Corvallis, where they spent the next 7 years while Tony was in school at Oregon State, and Gloria was busy with her three little Oregonians: Paul Hadley, Sherian Lynn, and Daniel John. Hey, they made of me a Grandpa and I loved it! We were camping and had this dear family to draw us to the West. After getting his degree, Tony and family lived in New Jersey for a few years, where he worked for DuPont. Now we could travel east to see them, Louise and Glenn in Rhode Island, and such places as New York City, Plymouth Rock, and the Atlantic Ocean. We have found that living in K.C. has the advantage of being equidistant to the two coasts. It was pretty handy since our kids have spread their wings.

Tony, Jeff, Mark and Tom holding their baby pictures 1971

It was also a time for Tony and Gloria to get to know Louise and Glenn, Cousin Phyllis and her husband Bob Dillsaver in N.J., and even get together occasionally with Jeff, Susan, Mark and Vicki for camping trips. Jeff and Mark were stationed in the East.

Tony loved the West and as soon as he could, he took his family to Idaho Falls, Idaho. The children grew up there and Gloria has become a highly acclaimed artist with many awards. She has been very successful in marketing her art. We have enjoyed decorating with the art works of Gloria. Tony has been happy in his work of energy research, both in research and as an executive.

In high school, Jeff was a good student and loved playing football. After graduation, he, too, worked a summer for the Forest Service in Oregon. We took him there and were with him on his 18th birthday as we felt he might need moral support when he had to register for the draft. The Viet Nam war was looming large. Several of our sons' friends were killed during that conflict. Jeff's draft number did come up while he was practice teaching in Atlanta, and he enlisted in the Air Force.

A friend introduced Jeff to Susan Curtis. We thank this friend to this day. They were married in 1967 and went to Nashville where Jeff was in Vanderbilt graduate school and Susan was in Geo. M. Peabody. He was sent to Atlanta to do his practice teaching, and Susan finished her degree at Georgia State. She was, and still is, beautiful.

These were frantic years for those two kids! The Air Force sent them to Lowell, Massachusetts, where Eric Curtis joined the family. After his tour of duty, Jeff went to Duke and then Southeastern to prepare for the ministry. He was ordained at the Methodist Conference in Virginia. After a few years in Kansas where the grandparents had an opportunity to know Eric and his little brother, Joel Harmon, and sister, Emily Elizabeth, the family returned to Virginia. Jeff rejoined his friends whom he had met at Duke. They had organized the Society of St. Andrew, an organization that gathers surplus farm produce and distributes it to the needy. Susan is also working with the Society of St. Andrew.

Mark was our gregarious boy. He did not know a stranger (took after his old Dad). After high school, where he had been a good wrestler, Mark went to Pittsburg State University. It was here he met pretty Vicki Feaster. He could not stay around to finish college and be with Vicki, because his draft number was drawn. He enlisted in the Air Force and spent two years in Turkey in Intelligence.

When Mark returned to the U. S., he married Vicki and they were stationed in Maryland for a year until the Air Force days were over. They returned to K.C. where Vicki started teaching (we need more good teachers like Vicki), and Mark finished his degree at Rockhurst College.

He is now working up the corporate ladder in the Post Office . Vicki and Mark have 3 children Zachary Douglas, Lindsay Brooke, and Kaitlyn Colby. They live in Marion, Iowa, close enough for us to drive. Zachary, who is a senior in high school, surprised us all when he announced that he had enlisted in the Navy at the close of the school year.

We appreciated having Tom still with us after Tony and Jeff were married and Mark was off in Turkey, but he found that being an only child had mixed blessings . The lawnmower and snow blower were now his exclusively, but he had no one to argue with concerning the use of the car. It was now a Ford LTD.

Celebrating Tom's 16th birthday at Lake Olallie in the Oregon Cascades. Back row George holding Grandson Daniel John, Gloria, Grandson Paul in front of George, Tom holding the Cake and Tony holding Granddaughter Sheri.

I was so happy and proud when Tom got his Eagle Scout award. His high school wrestling record made possible a wrestling scholarship at

Emporia State University. It was here he met the girl of his dreams, Janet Crowder. They were married and shared their senior years together at Emporia State. They are parents of Brian Alexander and Timothy Michael. Tom is an engineer on the Santa Fe Railroad and Janet keeps busy helping us. As a matter of fact we have appreciated having Tom, Janet, Brian and Tim available whenever we need them.

After having 2 Yorkshire Terriers, they now have a straight-eared, Scottish Fold Cat, named Lonesome George. I guess it is OK to share my name with a little creature as gorgeous as he is!

We have thought so often how our sons have enriched our lives by being what they are, and by giving us 4 wonderful daughters-in-law, who are like true daughters to us. The sons and "daughters" have further enriched our lives with 11 grandchildren and 5 great grand's! They are all the kind of citizens this world needs. Each one has a big spot in my heart.

So we're back to where we started, just Ruth and me. Louise and Glenn invited us to come back to visit in Rhode Island and go with them, in their camper, to such neat places as Cape Cod Canal. We found that the four of us were quite compatible, and Louise and I had a lot of catching up to do. They asked if we would share a rental with them in Florida. We all bought bicycles and golf clubs and had 12 years of "Fun in the Sun" on Anna Maria Island. The white sand beach and the friendships were unforgettable.

We used to drive on our long trips west to see Tony and Gloria, East to see Jeff and Susan, and south to Florida. However; we now find it is easier for Senior Citizens to fly. We still drive to Iowa when we visit Mark's family.

We no longer go to Florida as we have moved to Lakeview Retirement Village. We had built a house at 2511 N. 82nd Terr. KCK, which we thought would be our last home. But even that proved to require maintenance, so it was off to Lakeview where we are living it up with no responsibilities for house and yard and are surrounded by loving friends. Mary had lived here and had such good care until she died. Willardean is a neighbor of ours. It's fun to see her around here and at church.

50th Anniversary celebration for George and Ruth. Back Row: Mark, Tony, Jeff, Tom, Front: Ruth and George Allen

I said the house on 60th was our sons' home, but we found the house on 82nd Ter. was full of memories of grandchildren. We had a play room filled with Fisher Price toys and had so many happy parties in this house. We had Christmas celebrations when Jeff held a candle-light service. There were Thanksgiving dinners, Halloween parties, and birthday parties. We had Paul, Sheri, and Dan for a week as each reached the age of 16, and we got to know our far-away grandchildren a little better. That set a precedent and each grandchild began to have a time alone with us. They are all young adults now -except our little Katie, but our memories will never grow old!

George and Ruth on the Eureka Railway dining car during 1992 reunion at Table Rock Lake, George liked nothing better than to be with his family and second maybe was being on a train

In looking back, all I can say is; "What a life!"

LIFE GOES ON!!!

I thought I was through telling my story, but I just have to add another segment.

Ruth and I had planned to go to Idaho last September (1994). We had our tickets bought and bags packed. The day before our departure, my doctor called to say that I was going nowhere except to the hospital. In his examination, he had found a rather large aneurysm on my aorta, an extremely low blood count, and kidneys that had decided to claim partial retirement. So I started a 17-day stay at the hospital where they repaired the aneurysm and built up my red-blood count.

You can't keep a good man down, though, and we still had the airline coupons for tickets. Tony came up with the idea of our flying to Idaho to see the two new great-grandchildren there and after a week, he and Gloria would accompany us to Hawaii. Their daughter, Sheri, lives on Maui with her husband, Andrew, and year-old son, Frederick Locke Adolphsen. It seemed crazy, but Tony made the reservations. The time came for us to go and the doctor said: "Go for it!"

When we got to Idaho we met Dillon Robert David. He is the baby son of Michael and Kori David. I had not mentioned Michael in my story, but he is an important part of our family. As the unadopted son of Gloria and Tony, he makes the number of our grandchildren an even dozen. Little Dillon had scared his family when he was only 3 weeks old. He had congestive heart failure and had to be flown by helicopter to a children's' hospital in Salt Lake City. He was 3 months old when we saw him in February and he is the picture of a healthy, happy baby. His super mom is a nurse, good thing!

An even newer addition was tiny Taylor Valois Allen, the 6-week-old daughter of Paul and Janet. What a lucky little girl she is to have those two for parents. Besides having numerous grandparents, aunts, and uncles, she is particularly blessed in having a special loving sister, Challis, and two doting brothers, Daniel and Austin. She has quite a fan club to adore her and she is adorable!

We were sorry to have missed seeing Dan and Richelle. They would have been there if we could have made the trip in September, but such are the breaks!

I was feeling stronger each day, so we decided to continue on with our trip to Hawaii. When we got to Maui, we finally met our little Frederick who won us over immediately. Sheri and Andy made us feel so welcome. They showed us the attractions of the Island. We went to the top of Haleakala where we saw the huge crater. We saw the Protea farm with the beautiful large and colorful flowers. The little towns were so quaint. Our time on the beach was such fun as we watched little Fred playing in the big sand pile and his dog, Leda, chasing the Frisbee into the Pacific where she always retrieved it and swam back with it. We had a special day on a boat watching the whales. We just do not have that sort of thing in Kansas! Of course, Frederick was the main attraction on Maui. He let us read to him by the hour! It was hard to say good-bye to this dear family, but I came home with many memories. I'll never forget that it was Tony and Gloria who made it possible.

We are waiting for news of the success of Louise's cancer operation next Tuesday. If f can overcome my physical problems, surely my little sister can do no less. My prayers are with her.

9 ADDENDUM III

Photos and added information of the George Allen Family

The Levi and Jane Seybold Allen 40th Wedding Anniversay September 9, 1908
George Hadley Allen's Grandparents

Back Row: Harmon Allen, Amanda Allen Evertson, Minnie Allen McGee, Mae Allen Neal, man unidentified, Elsie Allen

Second Row: Mary Dunlap Allen with Mary Frances Allen on lap, Leah Hobson Allen, Levi Allen, Jane Seybold Allen, Charles Evertson with Russel Charles Evertson and Themal Allen Evertson on his lap.

Third Row: Norma Jane Evertson, Edna Lavina Evertson, Harriet Jane Allen, Ralph Therion McGee, Hazel Ester McGee, Nina Vera McGee

Front Row: Joseph Levi Dunlap Allen, Hazel Althea Evertson, Edward Harmon Allen, Harold Edmond Evertson, Hope Lorraine Neal, Raymond Walter McGee, Nina Vera Evertson, last two boys not identified.

Note: Harmon Allen's hand is on the shoulder of his Grandmother Leah Hobson Allen who was born in 1821

Levi Allen

Harmon and Mary wedding photo February 11, 1899

Harmon and Mary September 1923 in Leavenworth

Baby George **Allen about** 1914

Rev. Harmon Allen

Upper left: Edward and Willardean from an album of an elderly friend, Jenny Long, in Idaho Falls. Jenny remembered a Willardean from Campfire Girls and got out her photo album and showed Gloria this picture. Jenny recognized Willardean, but not the young man. Gloria exclaimed, why that is Uncle Edward. Jenny grew up in Lawrence, Kansas and apparently knew Willardean there.
Upper right: George Allen Sr. Ottawa HS
Bottom: Mary Dunlap in Biology class at Emporia Normal School, 2nd from left

Upper left: George at front door of Packard House on 32nd St.
Upper right: George holding Baby Tony
Bottom: George with baby Mark and Tony

Children of Harmon and Mary Allen plus Emma Dunlap, Mary's sister, From left: Edward, Mary Geiger, Emma Dunlap, George, Louise Rawlins, Harriett Noll, Joseph. Joseph died in 1949 so this photo had to be prior to that.

George with mustache grown to celebrate the Kansas Centennial with sons Tony, Jeff and Mark

George and Edward, 1950

George with baby Daniel John at Olalie Lake in the Oregon Cascade Mountains, 1958

George and Ruth clowning around at home in 1974

Ruth and George in Idaho in 1977. On the left they are ready for church. On the right they are on a Christmas Tree cutting expedition. Daughter-in-law Gloria memorialized this outing with a painting of George in his parka and fleece hat that hung in George and Ruth's house for more than 35 years. Dad's quote about that day was, "I have never been so cold."

George and Ruth visit John and Blanche Miller in Pensacola, Florida on their way to their winter retreat with Louise and Glenn Rawlins on Santa Maria Island, Florida 1980

My Common, Remarkable Family

Tony, Ruth and George during surprise visit Dec. 1980. Ruth began a tradition of making memory books for Tony's 40th birthday.

Dan, Paul, George on way to Grandson Paul's wedding. 1983

Allen family reunion Indian Point, near Branson, MO. From left: Eric, George, Ruth, Gloria, Tony, Joel in front of Tony, Dan, Emily in front of Dan, Tim and Brian in front of Janet, Tom, Susan and Jeff

George Allen on a boat on Lake Pend Oreille, Idaho 1985

My Common, Remarkable Family

George Allen, Idaho, 1988

WILL OF JOSEPH A. DUNLAP

KNOW ALL MEN BY THESE PRESENTS: That I, Joseph A. Dunlap, of Union Center Township in Elk County, Kansas, being of the age of Forty-nine years, and being of sound and disposing mind and memory and not being under any restraint or undue influence, do make and publish this as and for my last will and testament.

First: I direct that all my just debts be fully paid.

Second: I do give, devise and bequeath to my beloved wife, Harriett S. Dunlap, all my personal property of every nature or kind and whatever situated to be here absolutely to do with as she desires.

Third: I do give, devise and bequeath the possession, rents, use, issues and profits of all my real property where ever situated to my said wife, Harriett S. Dunlap until her death, provided she shall remain my widow and shall remain unmarried after my death, and upon her death, she then being my widow, I do give, devise and bequeath all my said real property to my children, Mary E. Allen, Emma M. Dunlap, Anna G. Dunlap, Nevada S. Dunlap, James H. Dunlap, Earnest C. Dunlap and Norwell Z. Dunlap in equal shares, in fee; and if my said wife, Harriett S. Dunlap, shall remarry, then and in that event, I do give, devise and bequeath one half of all my said real property to my said wife in fee, and the other one half of my said real property, in the event of the remarriage of my said wife, I do give devise and bequeath unto my said children in equal parts, in fee.

Fourth: I do hereby make and constitute my daughter Mary E. Allen executrix of this my last will and testament, and do request the she give no bond.

In Witness Whereof, I have hereunto signed my name, after the interlineations of the words, "she then being my widow" had been written in line 26 of the first page hereof, on the 16 day of March 1899.

                     (Signed)   Joseph A. Dunlap

PHOTO OF BEN LONG EAR

For years Dad told stories of Ben Long Ear and we all loved hearing them. Mark in particular enjoyed the knack of getting Dad to tell his stories with family all around him during family reunions. Ben Long Ear felt like part of the family and we have a leather purse he beaded for Aunt Harriett for her wedding in 1921. It resides in a box and needs some tender loving care and careful display to do it justice.

For several years Gloria and I wintered on the Olympic Peninsula of Washington State and Port Townsend captivated us on many excursions. One time we perused the Native American Art Gallery on Main Street. Upstairs in the gallery they had a number of books including one of Indian Photos by Edward S. Curtis, famous photographer of Indians during the early 1900s. You can imagine my surprise when I was thumbing through the book and found a photograph titled Ben Long Ear 1905.

The photo of Ben Long Ear on the next page was taken in 1905 when Edward S. Curtis photographed the Crow Indians. The photo above is his incarceration photo at McNeil Federal Penitentiary near Tacoma,

Washington found from McNeil Federal Penitentiary records on the Internet.

Ben Long Ear – Edward S. Curtis -- 1805

LETTER FROM GEORGE ALLEN TO ALICE ABOUT HIS FAMILY HISTORY

Dear Alice,

Ruth and I just returned from visiting Louise and Glenn. We had a wonderful time! They took us on a two day trip to Vermont. We visited Robe Lincoln's home. He was the oldest son of Abraham Lincoln. The home and grounds were beautiful. The next day we visited Calvin Coolidge's boyhood home. He was a very smart man and a much better writer than he was a speaker. So much past history packed into two days and I like history.

Alice, while we were at Glenn and Louise's they received a letter from you telling about Julia moving to a Rest Home. You mentioned that Julia remembers Ben Long Ear that she had met when Uncle Claude brought Julia and Mary to visit us.

Maybe Julia would like my memories of her visit and something about the full blooded Indian, Ben Long Ear.

As I remember Julia she was probably around 5 years old. She was pretty and cute and was busy all of the time doing her own thing. She didn't need anyone to play with especially a ten year old boy. I don't mean that she was unfriendly, she wasn't! I just couldn't keep up with her.

I'll give you a little bit of my background. I was five when I came to Leavenworth. Daddy was the Chaplin at the Federal Penitentiary. As Chaplin he was entitled to several prisoners to help around the house and yard. Mama didn't believe in having prisoners around us. She did agree to one yard man. The first one we had was Archibald Jones or Midnight as he was called. He was just as black as his name implied. With six children in the family Mama was pretty busy and so Midnight gradually began to ride herd on me. I loved that man and although Midnight was a crook he was always a gentleman around the family and me especially. Midnight was finally let out on parole.

Daddy was very much involved with the Indians. One of the things

Daddy did with the help of the Indians was to have an Indian Pow-Wow every Fourth of July. That was a big dance. One of the decorations that they had was a full sized Indian Tepee. Daddy took the Indians up the Missouri River to get willow trees. That is how I first met Ben Long Ear. Ben was the son of the fourth wife of the head Chief of the Crow Indian Tribe. As the son of a chief he was raised much like a prince would be raised in England. Ben was a tall man about six feet tall, straight as an arrow and a proud man. He could read and write and was a very good artist. He was excellent at handling animals of any kind.

When Midnight was paroled Ben was the next yard man. By that time I was about nine. I said that Ben was good at handling animals. He was equally good at handling a lively nine year old. With Ben it was a learning experience. He taught me a lot of the things that he would have taught a son of his own.

Ben was a very good story teller. He told me a lot of the old Crow legends. When he told a story he would get down on his haunches, take a stick and draw a map on the ground as he told the story. He told of the Crow tribe's hero's, their exploits in hunting, mainly buffalo. I do not ever remember him telling about battles between tribes. One of the Crow tribe's favorite animals was the fox. I won't say the fox was a God, but he did some superhuman things and was very smart.

I always loved animals, but he taught me how to raise animals. At one time I had a pony, a nanny goat, three dogs, 18 rabbits quite a number of pigeons and we always had a cow, pigs, chickens and Guinea Hens.

One time Ben found two squabs (domestic pigeons). He brought them home and he showed me how to soak corn and hand feed them by putting the corn in their beak and stroking their throat to make the corn go down. Mine was a brown and white squab and I named him McAdoo who was a politician that was the Democratic candidate for Vice President and Ben's a blue squab that we named Al Smith. Needless to say those two squabs became the start of the flock of pigeons that everyone hated.

The whole family loved Ben. Mary couldn't believe that Ben had ever done anything bad so she asked Ben why he was in prison. He said, "Because I killed a man." That is all Ben ever said about it. However, Daddy got a more detailed account of the crime at the prison.

Ben and his brother-in-law took the family wagon to town on Saturday. They got roaring drunk. On the way home the brother-in-law started to tease Ben. They got into a fight and Ben had a knife. The brother-in-law was a white man.

When I was about ten years old I started driving Joseph's Model T truck. He had rented a farm three or four miles out of town. Often he wanted something in town and he would send me in town for it and I used the Ford truck. Mama was deathly afraid of cars and she insisted that Ben go with me when I drove. Ben knew everything about a horse, but absolutely nothing about a car. So in the summer Ben and I spent a lot of time out on the farm. Ben could get me to work when no one else could. Joseph had a herd of cows that he was milking.

Joseph rented the farm from the Haggs. There were four Haggs. Mother Hagg was about sixy or better, Joe Hagg a son, Mrs. McDonald a daughter in her 40s and Stanley Hagg a grandson my age.

The Hagg family home burned while Joseph rented the farm. The house was rebuilt, but many keepsakes were lost. Mrs. McDonald couldn't accept the loss and she was in a deep depression and was suicidal. Also Joe Hagg, the son, had injured his back and was in a wheel chair.

Ben and I were cleaning out the cow barn when we heard a lot of screaming coming from the Haggs. We could hear Mrs. Hagg calling for help and also Joe Hagg calling. Ben and I started running toward the Haggs. We heard Mrs. Hagg yelling from the barn. Ben was a little bit ahead of me. There was Mrs. Hagg, a little old woman, in the barn next to the ladder in the hayloft holding up Mrs. McDonald around her knees. Mrs. McDonald, a big woman, had committed suicide by jumping out of the hay mow with a rope around her neck. Ben was up that ladder like a cat and untied the rope and had Mrs. McDonald down, but it was too late. By that time Joseph showed up and I was sent packing. The problem was Ben was off the reservation, and he was a prisoner.

The county sheriff had to be called. Joseph knew the sheriff and asked him to leave Ben's name out of the report which he agreed to do.

Ben had a lawyer working on his case trying to get him a parole. He was a full blooded Indian by the name of Yellow Tail. Ben finally got his parole. The only time I ever saw Ben excited was when he came to tell us his parole had come through. When Ben left to go back to the Crow Agency near Helena, Montana we never saw or heard from him again. Edward and Willardean went to Helena, Montana in the 1960's to see if they could find out anything about Ben. Ben was dead, but Edward talked to one of Ben's relatives. He said that Ben was a chief in the Tribal Council and had served in that position until his death.

So ends the story of Ben Long Ear.

By the way, one day I scratched my wrist when I was with Ben. He said he was going to make me a Blood Brother. He scratched his wrist. We put the two wrists together and the blood mingled and I was a Blood Brother of Ben's. He gave me the Indian name of Nutaba Cha Cher which means in the Crow language, White Bear. So I guess I am a Crow Indian!

Alice, as a little boy I lived a story book life. I had fourteen years of nothing but fun. Even the work was fun.

Some might think that being around prisoners is not a good place to raise a boy. My Mother didn't think it was a good place.

The Federal Prison at Leavenworth was a high class prison as prisons go. It was high class because of the type of prisoner. The types were bankers convicted of embezzlement, Doctors of medicine, Osteopathy, and Chiropractic. The medical professionals were mostly convicted of white slavery crimes. In those days if you took a woman across the state line for immoral purpose you could end up in Leavenworth. Anyone convicted of a crime in Washington D.C., any Indian living on a reservation and committing a crime was sent to Leavenworth Federal Penitentiary. The only place drug abusers could be treated in the U. S. was at Leavenworth. Daddy started a night school at the prison, First grade through High school. Practically all of the teachers were college graduates. Some of them had Master degrees and PhDs. Daddy's personal secretary had been vice president of a large bank.

Well Alice, I hope you will forgive me. When I get started on yesteryear, I don't seem to be able to stop.

If you write to Julia, tell her I do remember a cute little dark headed girl.

With love,

George[1]

---

[1] Uncle Claude was Claude Taylor husband of Sarah Nevada (Vada) Dunlap and Julia and Mary were their daughters. Julia was born in 1916. Alice was probably Mary Alice Dunlap, daughter of Earnest Charles Dunlap, brother of Mary Elizabeth Dunlap and Sarah Nevada Dunlap, so Alice and Julia would be first cousins. Alice was born in 1918.

Tony Allen

Harmon Allen Narrative of his marriage to Mary Dunlap, an interesting glimpse of live near the turn of the Twentieth Century

Our marriage Feb 11/ 1898
Mary Elizabeth Dunlap
and
Rev. Harmon Allen

On Friday evening we started from home to Howard where we were to be married the next day at noon in the M.E. Church. Miss Laura Moore who had been at the home sewing for a few days went with us to her home. It was very cold and we had a hot rock to our feet with three heavy covers over our laps. When we reached Howard about five o'clock we drove down to Mrs. Shelbys to give her an invitation, we then drove to Mrs. Thompsons where Miss Ettra Carpenter who was to be our Brides maid, was rooming. There, Mary stopped where she was to remain until time to rehearse at the church before services I drove at once to Grandma Wileys and left Marys suit and other things and also Miss Carpenters was satisfied for she was to come there the next morning to dress I then drove to the livery Barn and put up

My Common, Remarkable Family

I believe he is referring to the IOOF or the International Order of Oddfellows.

---

the team. at once, I hurried up to Fleek & Barkley's dry goods store to see Mr Barkley as he was to act as groomsman. I told him that we would be ready in a short time to practice at the church (It was now snowing and blowing bitter cold.) I went to the parsonage to see about the church and Bro. Horner thought it would be best to wait until after services, as the Presiding Elder was to preach and hold the Howard Quarterly Conference. I hurried then to Mrs. Thompson's to tell Mary and Miss carpenter that we would wait until after services to practice. Mary wanted us to go to the depot to get her dress that was to come by Express from Emporia. I went to the depot (bitter cold) and

There I left them and went over to the church to wait until the Quarterly Conference was over. Mr Bashford came over and waited with me. Soon as the services were over I went after Mary and Miss Carpenter. Soon after coming to the church Brother Colsen, the Presiding Elder, who was to marry us, drilled us a short time and then we adjourned. Mary and I went over to Grandma Wiley's (bitter cold) to stay over night. We found a great many presents. About eleven o'clock, we retired. The next morning, after breakfast, I went down to the Barber Shop to be shaved and have my hair dressed. After this I went to the depot again for the dress (bitter cold!!!) and received some presents to Mary. Went back the livery barn and asked one of the helpers to take Mary her dress and the presents. Then went to the P.O., transacted a little business at one of the stores and ordered the Buss to come after us at Grandmas at ten minutes of twelve. After ...

and at about eleven o'clock I went with Mr. Barkley to his house to dress and get ready. At 20 minutes of twelve and were ready and went over to Grandmas where we found Mary and Miss Carpenter ready. The Bus soon came but I had forgotten Mary's ring at Mrs. Barkleys and we had to drive around that way ...

Letter from Harmon to his wife Mary in the Hospital months before she died. It is a very tender and sweet letter.

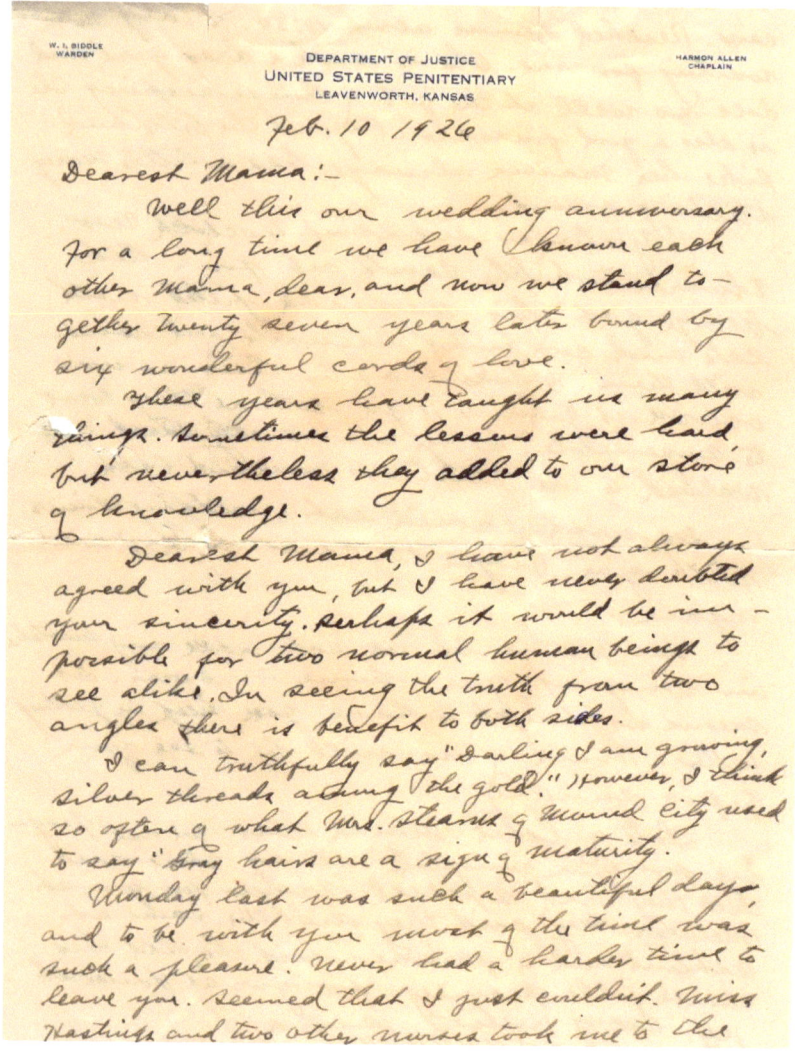

car. Reached home about 10:30. Mary was waiting for me. She is such a dear girl, and does so well at the job of housekeeping. She is also a good financier. Pays all the bills and like her mama always has a little money sticking around.

Yesterday eve about 4 o'clock Mr. Edwards took the scouts out for a hike. George got his napsack filled with eats and cooking utensils, and went with them. I went after him at nine o'clock at Junior High where they were to assemble. George was pretty tired. They walked to the Soldiers Home and back.

Do wish I could eat a wedding dinner with you. Maybe we can when I come again.

Now Mama let us not make any mistake in bringing you home too soon. It means so much to have you keep on getting better. Some of us will be to see you before Sunday.

Lots of love Mama dear. We are praying for your complete recovery. Elsie said that they had special prayer for you at Melvern. May said they did the same at Oakland, and a prisoner said he had his church folks praying for you at Louisville Ky. Many kisses Papa
ooooooooooo

Appendix

1. Underground Railroad Story and the part played by the Packard and Owen families.
2. Genealogy as understood by Georgiana Packard and family Revolutionary War Patriot Ancestors
3. Best available genealogy of and Ruth Allen's ancestors including Georgiana and George Washington Packard and their descendents as of 2014.
4. Best available genealogy of George Hadley Allen including early Virginians and possible link to King George III as of 2014.
5. Handwritten letter from Georgiana to her Mother-in-Law, Elizabeth Webster Packard, including a note from Georgiana's daughter Edith to her cousin Edith. May 27, 1877.
6. Handwritten letter from George Washington Packard to his mother. Last letter in Chapter 5.
7. George Washington Packard's Civil War Pay Records.

1 Underground Railroad Stories

The following story is from the book **John Brown** copyrighted in 1900 and written by William Elsey Connelley and put into digital form by Google. Georgiana provided the story to the author.

An account of John Brown, the Topeka Abolitionists including Cyrus Packard is described by the Kansas Historical Society.

That is followed by information about Cyrus Packard's Son-In-Law William Owen and an interesting story by Georgiana's sister, Olive.

Finally this appendix includes a story from the Topeka Capital-Journal about the burning of the Cyrus Packard House and includes photos of Georgiana's Granddaughter Ruth Packard Allen.

JOHN BROWN

BY

WILLIAM ELSEY CONNELLEY

Author of "The Provisional Government of Nebraska Territory," "James Henry Lane, the Grim Chieftain of Kansas," "Wyandot Folk-Lore," "Kansas Territorial Governors," etc., etc.

Sic itur ad astra

" From boulevards
O'erlooking both Nyanzas,
The statured bronze shall glitter in the sun,
With rugged lettering:

'John Brown of Kansas:
He dared begin;
He lost,
But, losing, won.'"

—*Eugene F. Ware.*

Crane & Company, Publishers
Topeka, Kansas
1900

332   JOHN BROWN

NOTE 11.—For accounts of the Marais des Cygnes massacre see *Kansas in 1858*, W. P. Tomlinson; and the account written for the Kansas State Historical Society by Ed. R. Smith, Esq., of Mound City, and published in the *Kansas Historical Collections*, Vol. VI, p. 365, and following.

NOTE 12.—This is given just as Brown wrote it. The original is in the library of the Kansas Historical Society. It was first published in the *New York Tribune* and the *Lawrence Republican*. The original shows some interlineations made with pen and some made with pencil. Mr. Sanborn believes those made with pen were made by Kagi. Mr. E. P. Harris was a compositor in the *Republican* office when the copy was received. The changes and additions made with pencil, now to be seen on the original, in the library of the State Historical Society, and the changes in orthography, were made by Mr. Harris, as he informs me. He also changed the punctuation. These changes all appear on the original copy in the handwriting of Mr. Harris. The paper as edited by Mr. Harris has been used as the copy of this valuable communication, and may be found in most all the biographies of John Brown. By comparing one of those with this the additions will readily appear.

The original paper bears some evidences that it was contemplated that some one else, probably Kagi, should make additions to it. There are spaces left to be filled if thought necessary; one of these follows the list of victims of the Marais des Cygnes massacre, and another is at the close. The only word in the original not in the copy as printed herein is the word "party." This is the last word, and is below the space and next to the signature. There is no connection between it and what precedes it in Brown's handwriting, and it is in his handwriting. Mr. Harris made it a part of the last sentence in the copy as published generally.

NOTE 13.—*Life of Captain John Brown*, James Redpath, p. 220.

NOTE 14.—Miss G. Packard, of Topeka, writes me:

"My father, Cyrus Packard, came from Maine to Kansas, in the spring of 1857. He lived about three miles north of Topeka, and John Brown frequently made his house his stopping-place, when traveling with slaves. I remember once, in the fall of 1858, that he came in the middle of the night with a large company, among whom was a babe who had been born on the road. My brother and I were little children, and were wakened in the night by the unwonted noise.

FAREWELL TO KANSAS 333

We got up and dressed and started to go downstairs, but found the door locked; and our curiosity was so great that we looked down through space around the stove pipe, and saw a great crowd of black people moving about. My brother-in-law, coming upstairs just then, concluded that we might as well be downstairs; so we were permitted to go about among the fugitives. I looked at John Brown with a great deal of interest. Col. Whipple and Kagi were with him. My mother and sister were bustling about, cooking as good a meal as they could under the circumstances. Before morning they were loaded into the covered wagons, and were well u𝑛 𝑟 way before daylight. Another time, word was brought to Topeka that John Brown was besieged by Missourians, and a company of men made a forced march to his relief. They suffered so much that by the time they got back they were entirely exhausted. One of them, one Captain Henry, came into my father's house and sank down. He was stricken with a violent fever and only lived a week, during which time he was unconscious. A friend of his, a Mr. Emerson from Topeka, helped take care of him, and closed his eyes for his last long sleep.

"This Mr. Emerson was quite a genius in his way. He was not a religious man, but was a very strong temperance man. He stammered in conversation. One time there was a company of fugitive slaves here, and there was a discussion as to how they were to be guided safely to the Queen's dominions. There was a plan that Mr. Emerson and Rev. L. Bodwell should impersonate Missourians, and take them through Missouri as their slaves. Mr. Emerson said to Mr. Bodwell, 'Y-y you c-can d-do the d-drinking, and I w-wi-will d-do the s-sw-swear-swearing.'"

NOTE 15.—*Life and Letters of John Brown*, F. B. Sanborn, p. 489.

NOTE 16.—*Life and Letters of John Brown*, F. B. Sanborn, p. 491.

About John Brown from Encarta Encyclopedia
Encyclopedia Article

John Brown (abolitionist) (1800-1859), called Old Brown of Osawatomie, American abolitionist, whose attempt to end slavery by force greatly increased tension between North and South in the period before the American Civil War.

Brown was born in Torrington, Connecticut. His family moved to Ohio when he was five years old. Early in life he acquired the hatred of slavery that marked his subsequent career, his father having been actively hostile to the institution. While living in Pennsylvania in 1834, Brown initiated a project among sympathetic abolitionists to educate young blacks. The next 20 years of his life were largely dedicated to this and similar abolitionist ventures, entailing many sacrifices for himself and his large family. In 1855 he followed five of his sons to Kansas Territory, then a center of struggle between the antislavery and proslavery forces. Under Brown's leadership, his sons became active participants in the fight against proslavery terrorists from Missouri, whose activities led to the murder of a number of abolitionists at Lawrence, Kansas. Brown and his sons avenged this crime, on May 24, 1856, at Pottawatomie Creek by killing five proslavery adherents. This act, as well as his success in withstanding a large party of attacking Missourians at Osawatomie in August, made him nationally famous as an irreconcilable foe of slavery.

Aided by increased financial support from abolitionists in the northeastern states, Brown began in 1857 to formulate a plan, which he had long entertained, to free the slaves by armed force. He secretly recruited a small band of supporters for this project, which included the establishment of a refuge for fugitive slaves in the mountains of Virginia. After several setbacks, he finally launched the venture on October 16, 1859, with a force of 18 men (including several of his sons), seizing the United States arsenal and armory at Harpers Ferry, Virginia (now West Virginia), and winning control of the town. After his initial success, he made no attempt at offensive action, but instead occupied defensive positions within the area. His force was surrounded by the local militia, which was reinforced on October 17 by a company of U.S. Marines under the command of Colonel Robert E. Lee. Ten of Brown's men, including two of his sons, were killed in the ensuing battle, and he was wounded and forced to capitulate. He was arrested and charged with various crimes, including treason and murder. He distinguished himself during his trial, which took place before a Virginia court, by his eloquent defense of his efforts in behalf of the slaves. Convicted, he was hanged in Charles Town, Virginia (now West Virginia) in December 1859. For many years after his death, Brown was generally regarded among abolitionists as a martyr to the cause of human freedom. He became the subject of a famous song, known generally by the first line as "John Brown's body lies a-mould'ring in the grave."

Battle of the Spurs

Published by the Kansas Historical Society

Kansas Historical Collections - Battle of the Spurs and John Brown's Exit from Kansas

by L. L. Kiene

1903-04 (Vol. VIII), pages 443 to 449

"Mother, John Brown has started for Canada with the Missouri slaves. Are there plenty of provisions in the house?" The speaker was Daniel Sheridan, who lived on an elevation two miles southeast of Topeka, the house commanding a view of the town and country for miles around. He had just returned from the village below, where, by some mysterious system known only to the men who conducted the underground railroad, he had heard of the movements of John Brown, which were guarded with careful solicitude by his friends and associates. The Sheridan home was the headquarters for John Brown when he was in the vicinity of Topeka. It was a small stone house, scarcely adequate for the Sheridan family of two members, but there was always room for Brown and as many fugitive slaves as were brought that way on their long journey to the country where the driver's whip and the strong hand of the United States government could not reach them.

The time was the latter part of January, 1859. The month had been an unusually mild one, with frequent rains and little snow, but the nights were by no means comfortable for travelers, and, where there was danger of detection, slaves were always moved in the night. The

Sheridan's, like other New England pioneers, had done their share in winning the struggle for race freedom in Kansas. But while Kansas had been saved from the slave-traders, the institution still existed, and these courageous reformers stood ready to give up their lives if they might by that means advance the cause of universal emancipation. John Brown knew that he could trust the Sheridan's. He had no fear that he would be betrayed while he was under their roof, and the house was so situated that the approach of officers of the law could be observed in time to get out of their reach, for not a day passed that there were not people on the lookout for John Brown and planning to secure his arrest. The aged emancipator had reached the period in life when his very name was a terror to the slave-owners and also to the local officers under the United States or the provisional government of Kansas. The president of the United States had set a price upon the head of Brown, and this had been supplemented by rewards by the governors of Missouri and Kansas. To the slavery sympathizers he was the red-handed murderer of innocent men who opposed him, but to the Sheridan's and other anti-slavery advocates he was a benign, fatherly individual, whose voice was seldom raised except in denunciation of human slavery.

It was therefore with no degree of fear, but rather a feeling of joyful duty, that the Sheridan home was made ready for visitors. The light was kept burning and an extra supply of wood was secured, so that a roaring blaze might be kindled in the expansive fireplace at a moment's notice. Mr. Sheridan then notified two of his intimate friends to be ready to receive visitors. One of these was Jacob Willits, who lived about a mile west of the Sheridan place, and the other was Col. John Ritchie, one of the most intrepid men that ever lived, whose home was in the village, at what is now Eleventh and Madison streets. Both these places were used as retreats for runaway slaves, as was also the William Scales residence, which stands in the heart of Topeka, near the corner of Fifth and Quincy streets.

The gray streaks of dawn were visible in the east on January 28 when the Sheridan's were aroused by a pounding on their door. To the inquiry, "Who is there?" a voice answered "Friends. Are you ready to receive visitors?" The man who awakened the Sheridan's was George B. Gill, who had left Garnett on January 20 as the only escort of John

Brown and the ten Negroes who had been captured in a raid into Missouri on December 20, 1858.

When the wagon which carried Brown and the slaves arrived the Sheridan's were waiting for them. The vehicle was what was known as a prairie-schooner, the type used by freighters, and which, while it served to conceal the contents, at the same time attracted little attention. The wagon was drawn by four horses, which had been substituted for oxen at Maj. J. B. Abbott's farm, five miles south of Lawrence, where a stop of several days was made for the purpose of selling the cattle and securing provisions for the long journey. There were twelve Negroes in the wagon when it drew up in front of the Sheridan home, a child having been born to the Daniels family while they were on the road. The negroes had all been taken from the Hicklan, Cruise and LaRue farms, in Missouri, and Cruise had been killed in the raid. It was Jim Daniels, one of the Hicklan negroes, who had told Brown that he with his family was to be sent South, which information had moved Brown and the anti-slavery men in his party to make a stroke for the relief of Daniels. The rescue and capture of the other Negroes had apparently been an afterthought. The slaves had little clothing when they were taken, and their condition had not been improved. When they arrived at the Sheridan place they were shivering with cold, as they were half clad and some of them were without shoes. They huddled down around the fireplace while Mrs. Sheridan prepared breakfast, and negroes and whites gathered around the little table and partook of a hearty meal. There was no caste at the Sheridan board.

After breakfast the fugitives were distributed among the trusted anti-slavery homes, and Sheridan, Ritchie and Gill went into the town to solicit shoes and clothing for the negroes. Brown was careful not to expose himself, and he remained all day at his retreat, where he paced the floor impatiently. He spoke occasionally to Mrs. Sheridan, and to her inquiry as to when he would leave, he replied: "We must be gone to-night. There is a great work before me--greater than I can tell, and you may never see me again, but you will hear." Mrs. Sheridan did not press the gray-bearded captain for more information, and did not know that a raid into the heart of the slave territory had been planned for the year before, and had been postponed because Brown had been betrayed by Hugh Forbes, who had acted as military instructor of the insurrectionists.

At dusk the horses were hitched to the wagon, and the negroes, who had been made more comfortable with clothing secured from the anti-slavery people, were gathered up. The sky was overcast and the wind was cold and chilling. It was not a pleasant night for a journey, but Brown would not wait for more propitious weather. J.H. Kagi and Aaron Dwight Stevens joined the party at Topeka and followed Brown to Virginia, where, with him, they gave up their lives--one, like him, on the gallows; the other a victim of the bullets of the infuriated people of Harper's Ferry.

Jacob Willits accompanied the travelers a short distance, and helped ferry them across the Kansas river. He stood beside Brown on the ferry-boat. The wind blew along the water from the north, rippling the surface and causing the aged emancipator to shiver. Willits noticed this and said: "I don't believe that you have enough clothes for this weather." "Do not bother about me. There are others not so well supplied," replied Brown

Willits then took hold of Brown's trousers and found that he wore no under-clothing, and after they had crossed the river he induced Brown to take those he wore, the exchange being made by the roadside.

A stop was made at the home of Cyrus Packard, four miles north of Topeka, where the negroes were unloaded and the refugees and their escort ate lunch. Holton was reached without incident at noon the following day, and the party took dinner at a hotel. They supposed that they had passed the danger point and no longer feared to travel in daylight. That afternoon, January 29, the prairie-schooner arrived at the log house of Albert Fuller, on Straight creek, six miles northwest of Holton. This was one of the stations on the underground railroad, and was situated in a community known to be in sympathy with the rescue of the slaves. It was agreed that the night should be spent at the Fuller cabin. The roads were bad on account of the rains, and the horses were jaded. Stevens went down to the stream after the negroes were safe in the cabin and was watering his horse, when he was suddenly confronted by two youthful deputy United States marshals on horseback.

"Have you seen any slaves around here?" asked one of the men.

"Yes," said Stevens. "There are some over there at the cabin now. I will go over with you."

The apparent frankness of Stevens threw the men off their guard, and one of them accompanied him to the cabin, while the other remained in charge of the horses. Stevens spent some time looking after his horse, to give the occupants of the house time to prepare an appropriate reception, and then he moved toward the cabin and threw open the door, saying, as he did so, "There they are. Go and take them."

The officer moved forward and found himself looking into the muzzles of two revolvers. A gruff voice said, "Come in here, and be quick about it," and he lost no time in obeying the summons. The young man was made a prisoner. The slaves were frantic with fear. After all, their sufferings had been for nothing, and they were to be recaptured and taken back to Missouri. Brown did his best to reassure them. "You won't be caught; we will take care of you," he said. But even then horsemen were gathering about a quarter of a mile off, near the creek, and the situation was far from reassuring. The invaders were careful to keep out of rifle range, but it was evident that their purpose was to capture Brown and his charges. The two men who accosted Stevens were a part of a posse under the leadership of John P. Wood, a deputy United States marshal from Lecompton. The company was made up principally of young men from Atchison and the surrounding country, and they were probably actuated quite as much by love of adventures as hope of reward. They were on the lookout for Brown, and were notified of his arrival at Holton. The terror with which the aged abolition warrior was regarded was never better illustrated than at this time. There were thirty or more men in the Wood posse, all well-armed and vested with authority of law. Opposed to them were Brown and his three associates and a few unarmed negroes. Still the officers were afraid to attack, and Wood drew up his forces in the shelter of the timber on Straight creek and sent for reinforcements.

Meanwhile Brown was not idle. One of the men crept out of the cabin under the cover of darkness, and went to the home of a farmer named Wasson, whose anti-slavery sentiments were well known, and he was requested to go to Topeka at once and tell Col. John Ritchie that John Brown was surrounded in the Fuller cabin, on Straight creek. Wasson lost no time in complying with the request. It was Sunday morning when Wasson reached Topeka. The little congregation was gathering in the schoolhouse, which stood at Fifth and Harrison streets, and which served as a meeting-place for the Congregationalists. Colonel Ritchie was already there and was waiting with his family for the opening of the services. A commotion at the rear of the building caused the people to turn their eyes toward the door as John Armstrong, one of the Topeka anti-slavery contingent, walked in excitedly and went to Ritchie's seat and whispered in his ear. Ritchie sprang to his feet and said audibly, "There is work for us," and strode out of the church with Armstrong.

The preacher, a young man named Lewis Bodwell, who had assisted in piloting more than one load of slaves out of the state, knew that something unusual had occurred, and he followed Ritchie and Armstrong. He soon returned to the church and made this strange announcement: "There will be no service to-day at this place. We will adjourn to the river bank."

The people filed hurriedly out of the schoolhouse and it was not long until the village was the scene of suppressed excitement and activity. The women were busy preparing provisions and clothing, while the men made a hurried canvass to find who could best leave home on what they knew to be a perilous journey. There were no protests from the women, though they knew that when they said good-by to their husbands and brothers it might be for the last time. Some degree of secrecy was maintained, because there were government officers in Topeka, and it was not deemed wise to let them know that a party was being organized to go to the rescue of John Brown, or even that John Brown was in the country. Much difficulty was experienced in finding enough horses, and when the dozen men left Topeka for Holton, some of them were on foot. In the party were Thomas Archer, John Armstrong, and Maj. Thomas W. Scudder, who still live in Topeka. They traveled all night, and the next forenoon, January 31, they arrived at Holton, where a half-dozen men and boys, including T.J. Anderson, now of Topeka, joined the Ritchie party, and they pushed on as rapidly as possible toward the Fuller cabin.

When they were within sight of the house they saw Kagi, Gill and Stevens hitching the horses to the wagon, and upon their arrival Brown was supervising the transfer of the negroes to the conveyance. Across Straight creek, a half mile away, were the horses of the Wood posse, and a line of dark mounds nearer the stream which marked the places where they had thrown up rude rifle-pits commanding the ford and the road leading to it. It had been raining, and the creek was high, and the Fuller crossing was known to be exceedingly bad.

"What do you propose to do, captain?" asked one of the body-guard.

"Cross the creek and move north," he responded, and his lips closed in that familiar, firm expression which left no doubt as to his purpose.

"But, captain, the water is high and the Fuller crossing is very bad. I doubt if we can get through. There is a much better ford five miles up the creek," said one of the man who joined the rescuers at Holton.

The old man faced the guard, and his eyes flashed. "I have set out on the Jim Lane road," he said, "and I intend to travel it straight through, and there is no use to talk of turning aside. Those who are afraid may go back, but I will cross at the Fuller crossing. The Lord has marked out a path for me and I intend to follow it. We are ready to move."

The members of the party exchanged glances of uneasiness, but when their eyes turned to the old leader he had already started toward the ford, and one by one they fell in behind him, and not a member of the party turned back. There were forty-five entrenched men waiting in their rifle-pits across the creek. Their guns were in their hands and directly in front of them, and not 100 yards away was the road leading to the Fuller crossing. They saw the little cavalcade of twenty-one men leave the cabin, preceded by a tall, lank figure, and they waiting in their entrenchments for their coming. The abolitionists moved out into the road and went straight toward the ford. Did the men who were waiting know that with a single volley they could wipe John Brown and his guard from the face of the earth? They certainly did, but what force was it that kept their fingers from their triggers? Perhaps the moral courage of the old man had paralyzed their arms.

John Brown appeared utterly oblivious of the presence of Wood and his forces. He looked straight ahead, and if the deputy marshal and his men had been ants they could not have received less attention from him. On toward the ford went the little company of Kansans. They did not fire a shot and not a gun was raised. As the advance-guard reached the ford there was a commotion in the rifle-pits on the opposite bank. A man or two sprang up and ran toward the horses, which were tied not far off, and in less time than it takes to tell it the entire marshal's party was in a wild panic, each member trying to outstrip the others in an effort to reach the horses. In their terror one or two of the men grasped the tails of the horses and were dragged over the prairie to a safe distance by the frightened animals.

The Topeka men charged across the creek to give chase, and found four men standing at their rifle-pits, apparently waiting for them. They had thrown their guns on the ground and stood with folded arms, awaiting the charge.

"Do you surrender?" shouted Colonel Ritchie.

"Yes, you may take us," said one of the men coolly. "We simply wanted to show you that there were some men in the Wood party who were not afraid of you."

The men were made prisoners, and their horses, which were tied nearby, were also taken. The heavy emigrant wagon became mired at the ford and it required several hours' work to get it through the creek. Then the march toward Tabor, Iowa, was resumed. The mounted members of the Topeka party, including Ritchie and Armstrong, accompanied Brown as far as Seneca and the rest turned back.

Thus ended the "Battle of the Spurs," which received its name from Richard J. Hinton, who belonged to the force of Eastern correspondents in Kansas. As spurs were the most effective weapons used, the title is not altogether inappropriate. Not a shot was fired on either side. If this encounter had not had its farcical termination there would have been no John Brown raid at Harper's Ferry in October of the same year, the world might never have known John Brown, the emancipator, and perhaps the institution of human slavery might have waited many years for its death-blow.

William Owen

WILLIAM OWEN. Much of the pioneer history of Kansas might be written around the names Owen and Packard. The late William Owen was one of the men who came from the East in the days of the '50s for the purpose of assisting in the movement to make a free state out of Kansas. His father-in-law, Cyrus Packard, was also a prominent leader in the free state movement.

Born in Rhode Island in 1827, William Owen came to Shawnee County, Kansas, in 1856, about the time the first territorial government was organized. As a young man in Rhode Island he learned and followed the trade of carpenter, and for a time was in the same vocation in Kansas. Later he conducted a sawmill, his being one of the first mills in the territory. He also was a merchant and kept a store at Rochester. After the war he was a farmer and carpenter, but in 1880 concentrated all his efforts upon farming and continued in that work for eighteen years, when he retired from business and moved to Topeka.

Mrs. William Owen before her marriage was Olive Packard, and the Packard and Owen families lived close neighbors after coming to Kansas. Her father, Cyrus Packard, who was born in the State of Maine June 5, 1796, served as a soldier in the War of 1812. He was a man of deep religious convictions, an active supporter of the Congregational Church and carried his religious beliefs and his social principles into practical action on every occasion. At the time of the abolition movement in Maine Cyrus Packard and one other man were the only ones in their community who had the courage to speak and advocate the cause openly. Cyrus Packard was nearly sixty years of age when the Kansas-Nebraska bill was passed and precipitated the conflict for a free state in Kansas. It was his ardent belief in abolition that caused him to abandon his comfortable home and come out to help make Kansas free.

William Owen was likewise zealously identified with the free state movement. At one time he was captured by the slave faction in Kansas and was taken to Lecompton and put in prison. A few days later the governor of the territory arrived at Lecompton, dined with the prisoner, and in a few days secured his release. Mrs. William Owen herself has many interesting anecdotes to relate concerning early days in Kansas. She recalls the fact that John Brown stopped one night at the Owen house with sixteen negroes, and Brown was not an infrequent visitor at the Owen or Packard homes. In fact everyone associated with the old underground railroad knew the Owen and Packard families. General W. T. Sherman when a young man managing the Thomas Ewing ranch boarded with the Owen family and the general with Mr. Owen's assistance built what was known for many years as the Sherman cabin.

Mr. and Mrs. Owen had fourteen children, six sons and eight daughters. Ten of these children are still living.

Transcribed from volume 4, pages 1764-1765 of **A Standard History of Kansas and Kansans**, written and compiled by William E. Connelley, Secretary of the Kansas State Historical Society, Topeka. Chicago: Lewis Publishing Company, copyright 1918; originally transcribed 1998, modified 2003 by Carolyn Ward.

Olive Packard Owen - Early Days in Kansas

As one of the pioneer women of Kansas, I have been asked to relate some personal reminiscences of John Brown, General Sherman, the Indians and some of my experiences of the early days.

My experience in Kansas began about four years before the Civil War. My father, who was one of the earliest abolitionists, hearing of the border troubles in Kansas, decided to leave his home in Maine and come to help settle Kansas as a free state. As I was fifteen years old the year we came I remember quite distinctly our trip. We came by rail to Jefferson City, then took the boat and came up the Missouri River and landed at Quindaro, a place near Kansas City, in April, 1857. From there we had to hire a man to bring us by wagon to our destination, which was the home of my brother-in-law, William Jordon, three miles south of Topeka. Topeka at this time was a village of only 60 buildings. This trip of sixty miles which now can be made by auto in two or three hours, took us two days and cost us twenty-five dollars for the conveyance alone, beside the expense of the stay overnight. As there were no hotels on the way, we spent the night at an Indian shack. I remember I didn't relish the food as I imagined the meat must be dog meat, since I had heard that was what the Indians ate. And the sight of the squaw, barefoot, didn't help my appetite as it was the first time I had ever seen a woman go barefoot. The expense of this trip almost depleted my father's purse; for although a good latin student, and having spent thirty years of his life teaching school, he had never accumulated much of the world's goods. So we landed at our destination with only fifty dollars.

To help out financially, as well as to do something for the country, it was decided that I might teach school. Although only fifteen, I was old for my age, and had completed common school and had taken some work at the academy. There were no public schools here, of course, at this time. This private school I thought was, as far as I know, the first school taught in Shawnee County. It happened my brother-in-law, Jesse Stone, had built a frame house and so there was a vacant an old log house in which they had been living. Stone said we might have this for a school house. The men fixed up seats of blocks of woodsplit, with sticks for legs. Of course there were no desks. Then I went around the neighborhood and gathered children for a subscription school. The parents couldn't afford to pay me much money, so I was supposed to board around as part of my remuneration. The great trial in this was that one family was a family of mulattoes. The father was a French man and the mother a Negro. I had to take my turn at staying there for fear of offending them. As we had never before seen negros before we came to Kansas I was naturally prejudiced. But my experience there was most pleasant. I was given a spare room, waited upon and treated like a queen, and fed upon the choicest of foods; for "Black Ann", as the woman was known, was a famous cook. I remember once having to dismiss the school long enough to kill a snake that was crawling up through the logs. Some of the pupils of this first school of Shawnee County are now among the leading men of the state.

I taught school only one year, as I was married when I was sixteen to William Owen, who came to Kansas a year earlier than our family. My husband was also a strong abolitionist and with my father and mother, established what was known as one of the stations of the Underground Railroad. Here, John Brown often stopped with slaves he was piloting thru to freedom in the North. The last time he came he had sixteen slaves and was traveling with them in a covered wagon. They arrived after dark. John Brown came to the door to inquire if there was anyone there except the family. On finding there was not, he drove the wagon in some brush back of the house and slept there a few hours, starting off again before daylight. Before they left my mother and I got up and cooked their breakfast, which consisted mostly of cornbread. I remember they all sat down at a long table with John Brown at the head. A little colored baby had been born on the way, and they had christened him John Brown.

It was on this trip that John Brown with his slaves was overtaken near Holton by some slave holders. But Brown and his party overpowered the slave holders and held them prisoner until he sent back to Topeka for help. Several men went up to help him and succeeded in sending the slave holders back home. It was related by the slave holders themselves that before releasing them, John Brown, at the point of a gun, forced them to kneel and say a prayer.

This same year General Sherman boarded with us for a week, while he was overseeing some buildings. I remember he was a very pleasant man, and how he delighted me a young wife, by bragging on my cooking.

Many exciting and interesting experiences happened to us in those early days. In those early times one of our great dreads was prairie fires. I remember one instance quite distinctly. My husband was making sorghum molasses. He had a force that stripped out the cane and boiled a barrel of sorghum a day. About four o'clock in the afternoon, we saw the smoke rolling up in the northwest. We had a farm about a mile and a half northwest with a shanty and several stacks of hay that would be in the path of the fire. My husband at once gathered some men and with a plow and some gunny sacks, they went as fast as they could to fight the fire. And I was left to boil molasses. I had to keep up the fire and when the sorghum was done, put out the fire and cover the molasses until morning. This boiling was not quite as thick as it should have been but at least it didn't burn. The men came back after a hard night's work but they succeeded in saving the hay and the house. In those early days men often took the law in their own hands. I remember one instance in particular, when a neighbor had an almost ungovernable temper, and had taken out after a thief with a gun. The thief ran right into our house and I was the only one there. The man with the gun was going to enter right after him, saying he was going to kill him. I happened to have an old revolver and I grabbed it, and holding it told the man he could not enter the house with that gun. Although the revolver was empty, it served to bring the man to his senses, and he consented to wait and let the law take its course.

I should have explained that during these experiences we were living at Rochester, two miles north of Topeka. Many Kaw Indians were living in that vicinity at that time. While as a rule they were not dangerous, they were a source of constant worry and much bother. They were great beggars. It was no uncommon sight to look up and see the door and windows full of Indians crying "hunger", "hunger" which meant they wanted something to eat. They would come into the house and beg for clothes, also. On one occasion when a company of them surrounded the house I was cooking dinner for the men who were building a bridge across Soldier Creek. I had just put my dinner on to cook when they came swarming around the house calling "hunger". I thought with dismay there would be no dinner left for the men that day. But I learned that "pocachee" meant for them to leave, and I said it pretty lively, and they left and saved my dinner for the men. It was only when they were drunk that we really needed to fear them. But as they often stopped on their way back from Topeka it was not uncommon to see them drunk. On one occasion a drunken Indian came into my husband's store in Rochester, flourishing a knife. Mr. Owen gave a leap over the counter, grabbed him by the elbows and pinned his arms behind his; thus averting what otherwise might have been a bad accident or serious tragedy.

These are only a few instances that went to make our early life in Kansas an interesting and often arduous adventure.

Mrs. William Owen

Tony Allen

Burned house harbored slaves

2006 FILE PHOTOGRAPH/THE CAPITAL-JOURNAL

The historic Owen house north of Topeka — once a stop on the Underground Railroad — may not have been destroyed in a fire this past weekend.

DOCUMENTS

Read Early Days in Kansas and The Underground Railroad, both written by Olive Owen, and Leaves from the Life of a Kansas Pioneer, which was written by Georgiana Packard for her children.

Original part of house still in 'good shape'

BY MIKE HALL

Created October 19, 2009 at 4:42pm
Updated October 20, 2009 at 12:21am

Local historians were rejoicing Monday that the historic Owen house north of Topeka -- a stop on the Underground Railroad -- may not have been destroyed by fire over the weekend after all.

Dee Puff, a local historian, said she visited the site Monday and found the original part of the house, built about 1856, remained in "really good shape." She said the owner, Jack DeBacker, was planning to have it evaluated to determine whether it could be restored.

"The newer part didn't fare as well as the older part," she said.

Puff was instrumental in getting the National Park Service to certify the Owen house, 3212 N.W. Rochester Road, as a place that actually harbored slaves as they were escorted to freedom in Canada before the Civil War.

The cause of the fire is being recorded as "undetermined" by the Kansas State Fire Marshall's office. However, since no evidence to the contrary was found, "it's more likely than not accidental," said Rose Rozmiaek, chief of investigation.

Information supplied by Puff and by Sylvie Rueff, of Lawrence, describe the history of a remarkable family of abolitionists who moved to Kansas in the 1850s.

Rueff is a great-great-great-granddaughter of Cyrus and Sarah Packard. Much of what is known about the Packard and Owen families comes from memoirs written by their daughter Olive in 1909 or later.

The two-story house was first constructed in 1856 or 1857 by William Owen. Originally it was "two rooms down and two rooms up," Puff said. Soon the front lower level was used as a general store or trading post to serve a small community most often known as Rochester. However, Puff noted it "changed names four times and counties twice."

Rueff said Owen appears to have owned the house for many years, even after he allowed Cyrus Packard's family to occupy it in 1857.

Then in 1858, Owen became the Packards' son-in-law.

"It is unclear whether Olive and William lived in the house after their marriage late in 1858," Rueff said. "It is always referred to as Cyrus Packard's home in stories of the Battle of the Spurs."

In one of Olive's later memoirs, she described a night, apparently in January 1859, when John Brown showed up at the house and asked the Packards for a place to sleep for a group of slaves and their escorts. Sarah Packard was asked to prepare a breakfast early enough that the group could leave for the next way station before dawn.

"This would be Brown's last trip through Shawnee County," Puff said.

In October 1859, Brown led an unsuccessful raid on a federal arsenal at Harper's Ferry, Va. He was captured and hanged in December.

Mike Hall can be reached at (785) 295-1209 or mike.hall@cjonline.com

Ruth and son Tony standing in front of the William and Olive Owen House in 2011, near to the home of Cyrus Packard. Both the Packard's and the Owens were active in the abolition movement and welcomed John Brown when he transported slaves to Canada and freedom. Ruth's visit was 153 years after Georgiana described her looking down from the second floor onto John Brown and a group of escaping slaves. Since William Stone allowed Cyrus Packard and his family to occupy the house in 1858, this is likely the house Georgiana described here that John Brown visited.

Transcribed from *A Standard History of Kansas and Kansans*, written and compiled by William E. Connelley, Secretary of the Kansas State Historical Society, Topeka. Chicago: Lewis Publishing Company, copyright 1918

2. Packard Genealogy by Georgiana Packard

Georgiana Packard

Georgiana Packard's parents were Cyrus Packard and Sarah Barrows. His father was Ichabod Packard and his mother was Rachel Cole. Through Rachel Cole there are at least four lines to passengers who came over in the Mayflower, which landed at Plymouth in 1620. They are Richard Warren, James Chilton, Edward Winslow and John Alden and Priscilla Mullins.

Edward Winslow

Edward Winslow was a passenger on the Mayflower. His son, John married Mary Chilton, the daughter of James Chilton a passenger on the Mayflower. Their daughter, Mary married Edward Gray. Their daughter, Susannah, married John Cole. Their son, Joseph Cole, married Mary Stevens in 1729, the great grandparents of Rachel Cole. Rachel Cole married Ichabod Packard in 1786. Their son, Cyrus Packard, married Sarah Barrows, the parents of Georgiana Packard.

Richard Warren

Richard Warren was a passenger on the Mayflower. His daughter, Amy married Robert Bartlett, who came over in "The Anne" in 1623. Their daughter Mary Bartlett was married in 1625 to Eleazer Churchill, who was born in 1652. Their daughter Mary Churchill married Edward Joseph Cole in 1729. He was born in 1700. Their son, Ephraim Cole, (born in 1731) married Hannah Randall in 1750 (Hannah Randall's father, Thomas married Hannah Packard, granddaughter of Samuel Packard, first passenger to come over 1638). Ephraim Cole and Hannah Randall were the parents of Joseph Cole, the father of Rachel Cole.

John Alden

John Alden, a passenger on the Mayflower, married Priscilla Mullins. Their daughter, Elizabeth married William Pabodie, Dec. 26, 1644. Their daughter married John Churchill. Their son Eleazer Churchill, born 1652, married Mary Bartlett in 1675, whose daughter Mary, married Edward Stevens and was the great great grandmother of Rachel Cole.

Several other lines to the Mayflower may be traced through the Packards and William Barrows – the founder of Hebron Academy and a Revolutionary Patriot.

Among the Revolutionary Patriot ancestors are:

- Ichabod Packard
- Reuben Packard
- Ephraim Cole
- William Barrows

*A more accurate genealogical record is included in the appendix.

3. Best available Genealogy for Ruth Packard Allen

George and Ruth Allen's descendents and Ruth's Ancestors through Georgiana and George Washington Packard and to the Pilgrims and Mayflower Passenger Richard Warren through Sarah Barrows. Also shows early Massachusetts arrivals including Ensign Samuel Packard and others who immigrated from England through Holland in the early 1600s.

Tony Allen

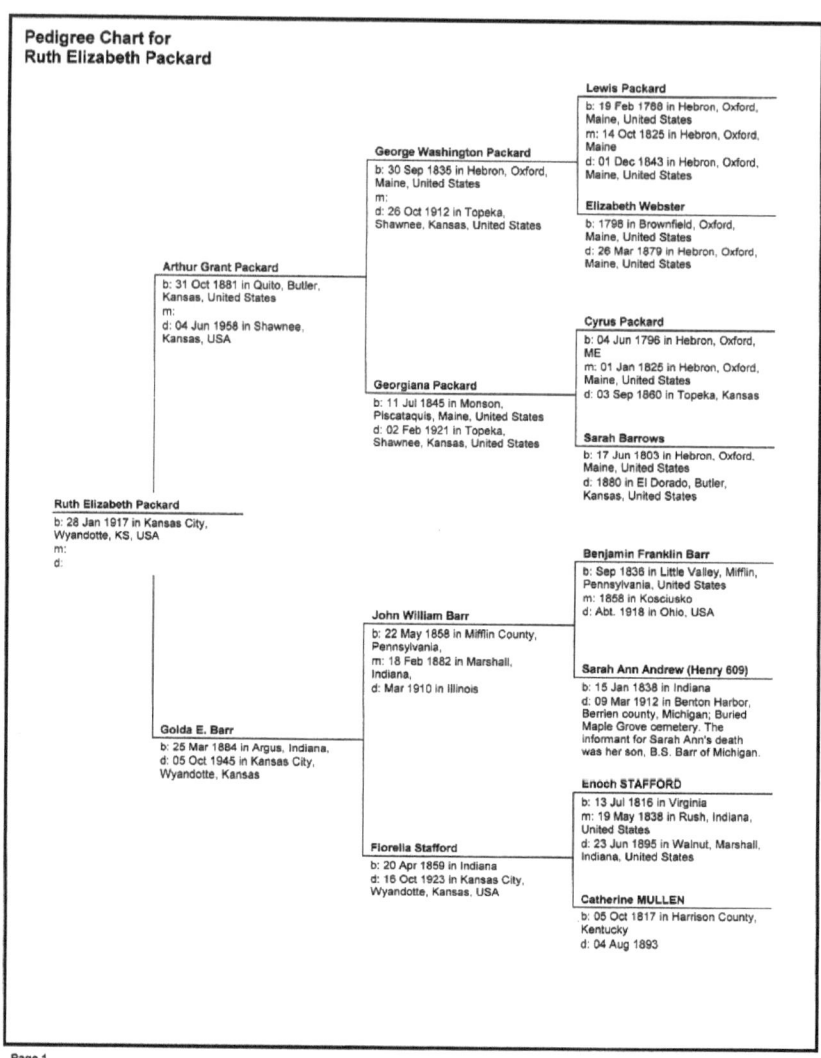

My Common, Remarkable Family

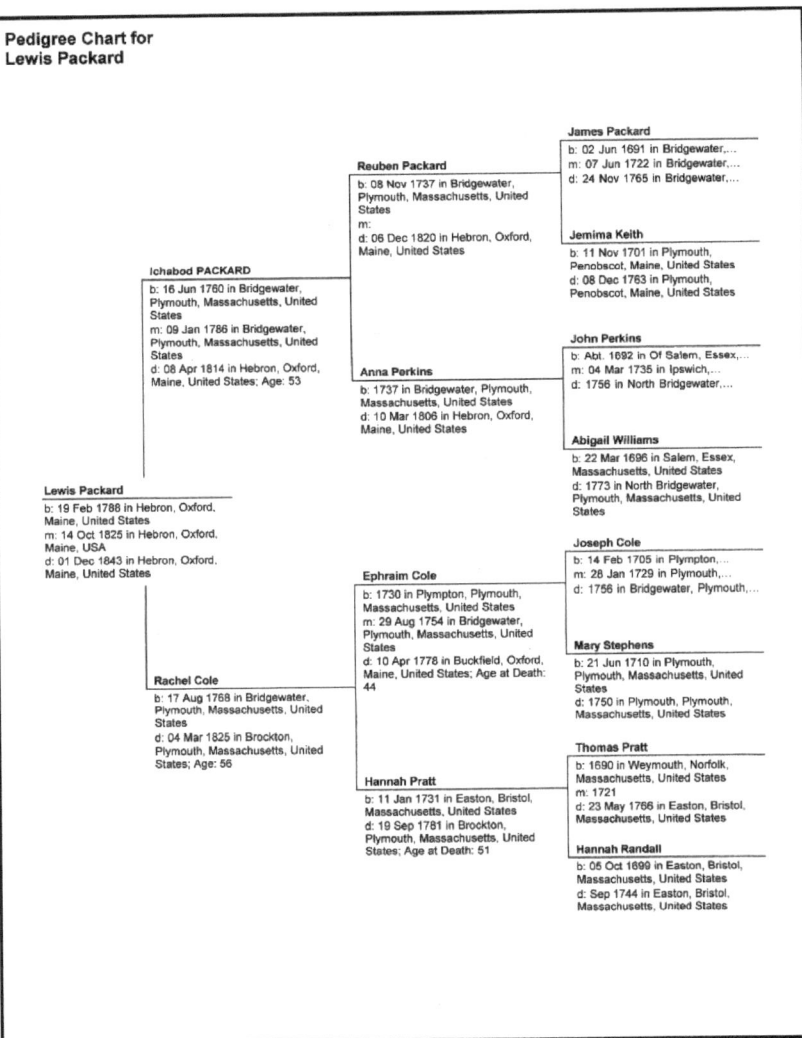

Tony Allen

Pedigree Chart for Cyrus Packard

Cyrus Packard
b: 04 Jun 1796 in Hebron, Oxford, ME
m: 01 Jan 1825 in Hebron, Oxford, Maine, United States
d: 03 Sep 1860 in Topeka, Kansas

- **Ichabod PACKARD**
  b: 16 Jun 1760 in Bridgewater, Plymouth, Massachusetts, United States
  m: 09 Jan 1786 in Bridgewater, Plymouth, Massachusetts, United States
  d: 08 Apr 1814 in Hebron, Oxford, Maine, United States
  - **Reuben Packard**
    b: 08 Nov 1737 in Bridgewater, Plymouth, Massachusetts, United States
    m:
    d: 06 Dec 1820 in Hebron, Oxford, Maine, United States
    - **James Packard**
      b: 02 Jun 1691 in Bridgewater,...
      m: 07 Jun 1722 in Bridgewater,...
      d: 24 Nov 1765 in Bridgewater,...
    - **Jemima Keith**
      b: 11 Nov 1701 in Plymouth, Penobscot, Maine, United States
      d: 08 Dec 1763 in Plymouth, Penobscot, Maine, United States
  - **Anna Perkins**
    b: 1737 in Bridgewater, Plymouth, Massachusetts, United States
    d: 10 Mar 1806 in Hebron, Oxford, Maine, United States
    - **John Perkins**
      b: Abt. 1692 in Of Salem, Essex,...
      m: 04 Mar 1735 in Ipswich,...
      d: 1756 in North Bridgewater,...
    - **Abigail Williams**
      b: 22 Mar 1696 in Salem, Essex, Massachusetts, United States
      d: 1773 in North Bridgewater, Plymouth, Massachusetts, United States
- **Rachel Cole**
  b: 17 Aug 1768 in Bridgewater, Plymouth, Massachusetts, United States
  d: 04 Mar 1825 in Brockton, Plymouth, Massachusetts, United States
  - **Ephraim Cole**
    b: 1731 in Plympton, Plymouth, Massachusetts, United States
    m: 29 Aug 1754 in Bridgewater, Plymouth, Massachusetts, United States
    d: 1775 in Buckfield, Oxford, Maine, United States
    - **Joseph Cole**
      b: 14 Feb 1706 in Plymouth,...
      m: 28 Jan 1729 in Plymouth,...
      d: 1777 in Bridgewater, Plymouth,...
    - **Mary Stephens**
      b: 21 Jun 1710 in Plymouth, Plymouth, Massachusetts, United States
      d: 1750 in Plymouth, Plymouth, Massachusetts, United States
  - **Hannah Pratt**
    b: 11 Jan 1731 in Easton, Bristol, Massachusetts, United States
    d: 19 Sep 1781 in Brockton, Plymouth, Massachusetts, United States
    - **Thomas Pratt**
      b: 1690 in Weymouth, Norfolk, Massachusetts, United States
      m: 1721
      d: 23 May 1766 in Easton, Bristol, Massachusetts, United States
    - **Hannah Randall**
      b: 05 Oct 1699 in Easton, Bristol, Massachusetts, United States
      d: Sep 1744 in Easton, Bristol, Massachusetts, United States

My Common, Remarkable Family

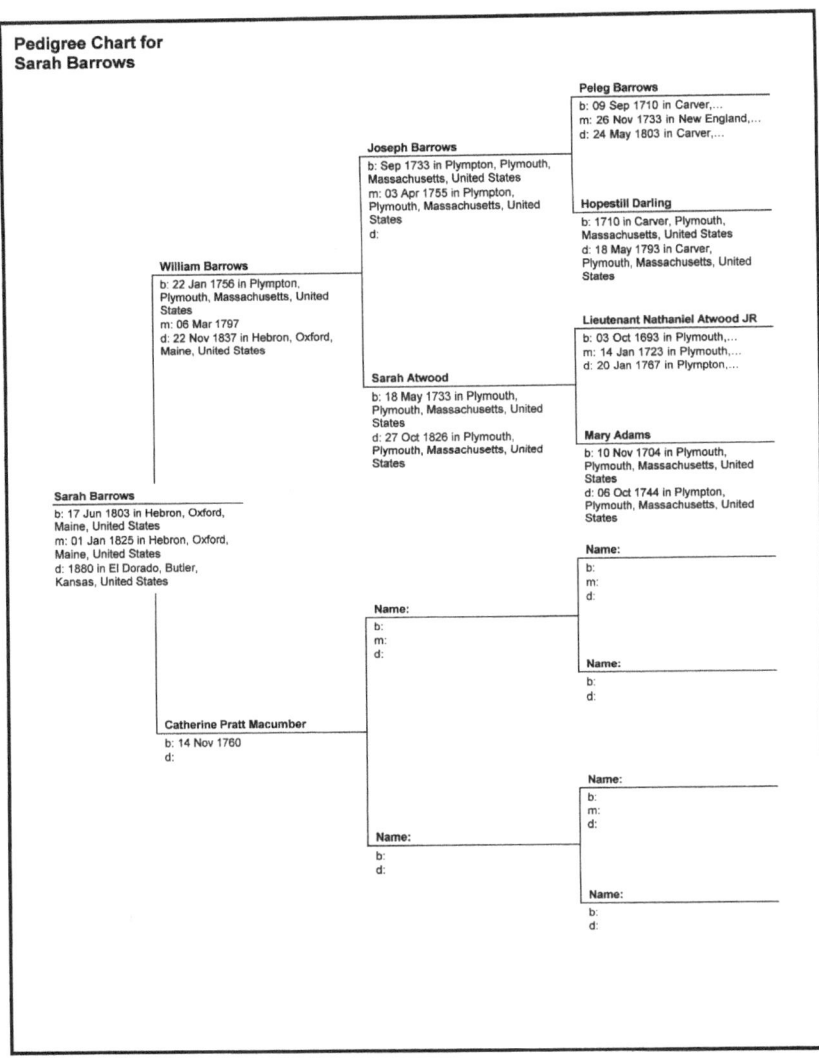

Pedigree Chart for Sarah Barrows

- **Sarah Barrows**
  b: 17 Jun 1803 in Hebron, Oxford, Maine, United States
  m: 01 Jan 1825 in Hebron, Oxford, Maine, United States
  d: 1880 in El Dorado, Butler, Kansas, United States

  - **William Barrows**
    b: 22 Jan 1756 in Plympton, Plymouth, Massachusetts, United States
    m: 06 Mar 1797
    d: 22 Nov 1837 in Hebron, Oxford, Maine, United States

    - **Joseph Barrows**
      b: Sep 1733 in Plympton, Plymouth, Massachusetts, United States
      m: 03 Apr 1755 in Plympton, Plymouth, Massachusetts, United States
      d:

      - **Peleg Barrows**
        b: 09 Sep 1710 in Carver,...
        m: 26 Nov 1733 in New England,...
        d: 24 May 1803 in Carver,...

      - **Hopestill Darling**
        b: 1710 in Carver, Plymouth, Massachusetts, United States
        d: 18 May 1793 in Carver, Plymouth, Massachusetts, United States

    - **Sarah Atwood**
      b: 18 May 1733 in Plymouth, Plymouth, Massachusetts, United States
      d: 27 Oct 1826 in Plymouth, Plymouth, Massachusetts, United States

      - **Lieutenant Nathaniel Atwood JR**
        b: 03 Oct 1693 in Plymouth,...
        m: 14 Jan 1723 in Plymouth,...
        d: 20 Jan 1767 in Plymouth,...

      - **Mary Adams**
        b: 10 Nov 1704 in Plymouth, Plymouth, Massachusetts, United States
        d: 06 Oct 1744 in Plympton, Plymouth, Massachusetts, United States

  - **Catherine Pratt Macumber**
    b: 14 Nov 1760
    d:

Page 1

251

Tony Allen

Pedigree Chart for Lieutenant Nathaniel Atwood JR

Lieutenant Nathaniel Atwood JR
b: 03 Oct 1693 in Plymouth, Plymouth, Massachusetts, United States
m: 09 Oct 1747 in Plymouth, Plymouth, Massachusetts, United States
d: 20 Jan 1767 in Plympton, Plymouth, Massachusetts, United States

- **Nathaniel Atwood**
  b: 25 Feb 1651 in Plymouth, Plymouth, Massachusetts, United States
  m: 1683 in Plympton, Plymouth, Massachusetts, United States
  d: 17 Dec 1724 in Plymouth, Plymouth, Massachusetts, United States
  - Name:
    b:
    m:
    d:
    - Name:
      b:
      m:
      d:
    - Name:
      b:
      d:
  - Name:
    b:
    d:
    - Name:
      b:
      m:
      d:
    - Name:
      b:
      d:

- **Mary Morey Lucas**
  b: 25 Feb 1650 in Plymouth, Plymouth, Massachusetts, United States
  d: 05 Dec 1736 in Plympton, Plymouth, Massachusetts, United States; Age at Death: 76
  - **Jonathan Morey Lt.**
    b: 02 Apr 1633 in Salem, Essex, MA
    m: 08 Jul 1659 in Plymouth, Plymouth, Massachusetts, United States
    d: 19 May 1708 in Plymouth, Plymouth, Massachusetts, United States; Age: 71
    - **Roger MOWRY**
      b: 1612 in Roxbury, Suffolk, England
      m: 1639 in Roxbury, Suffolk, Massachusetts, United States
      d: 05 Jan 1666 in Salem, Essex, Massachusetts, USA
    - **Mary JOHNSON**
      b: 31 Jul 1614 in Herne Hill, London, England
      d: 29 Jan 1678 in Rehoboth, Bristol, Massachusetts, United States
  - **Mary Bartlett Foster Morey**
    b: 1633 in Plymouth, Plymouth, Massachusetts, United States
    d: 26 Sep 1692 in Milton, Norfolk, Massachusetts, United States
    - **ROBERT BARTLETT**
      b: 27 May 1603 in Puddleton,...
      m: 22 May 1627 in Plymouth,...
      d: 19 Sep 1676 in Plymouth,...
    - **Mary Warren 10**
      b: 1609 in Greenwich, London, England
      d: 27 Mar 1683 in Northampton, Hampshire, Massachusetts, United States

Page 1

My Common, Remarkable Family

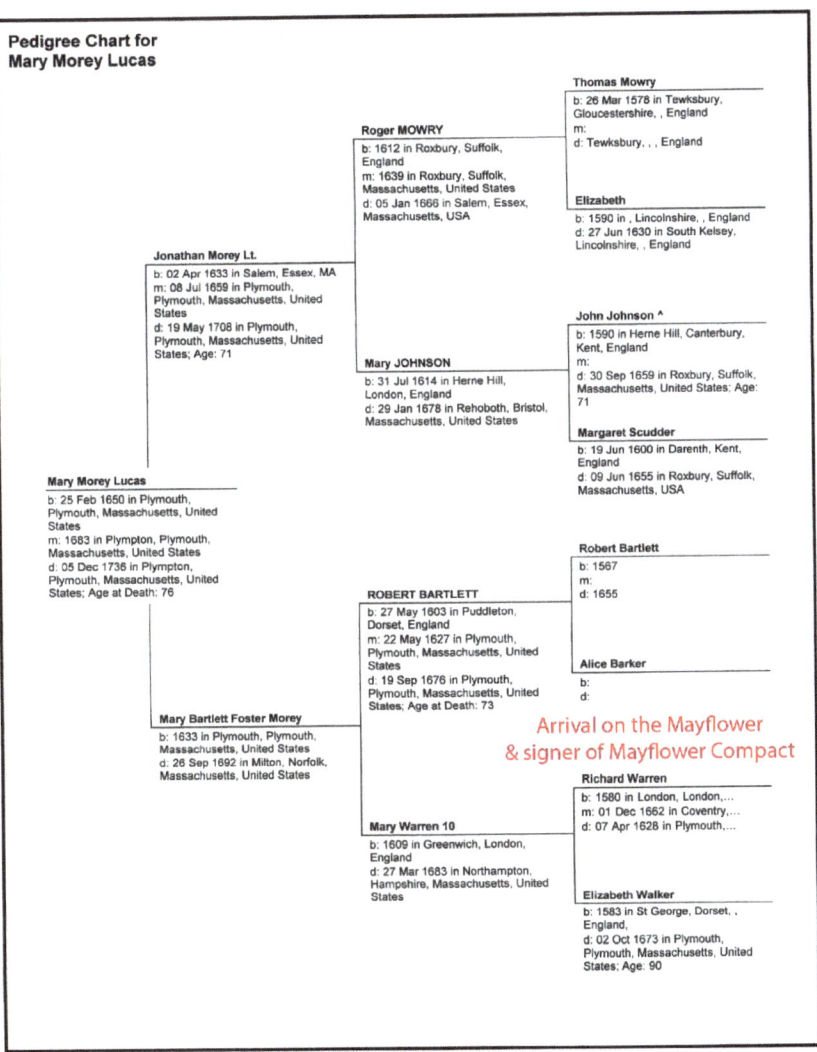

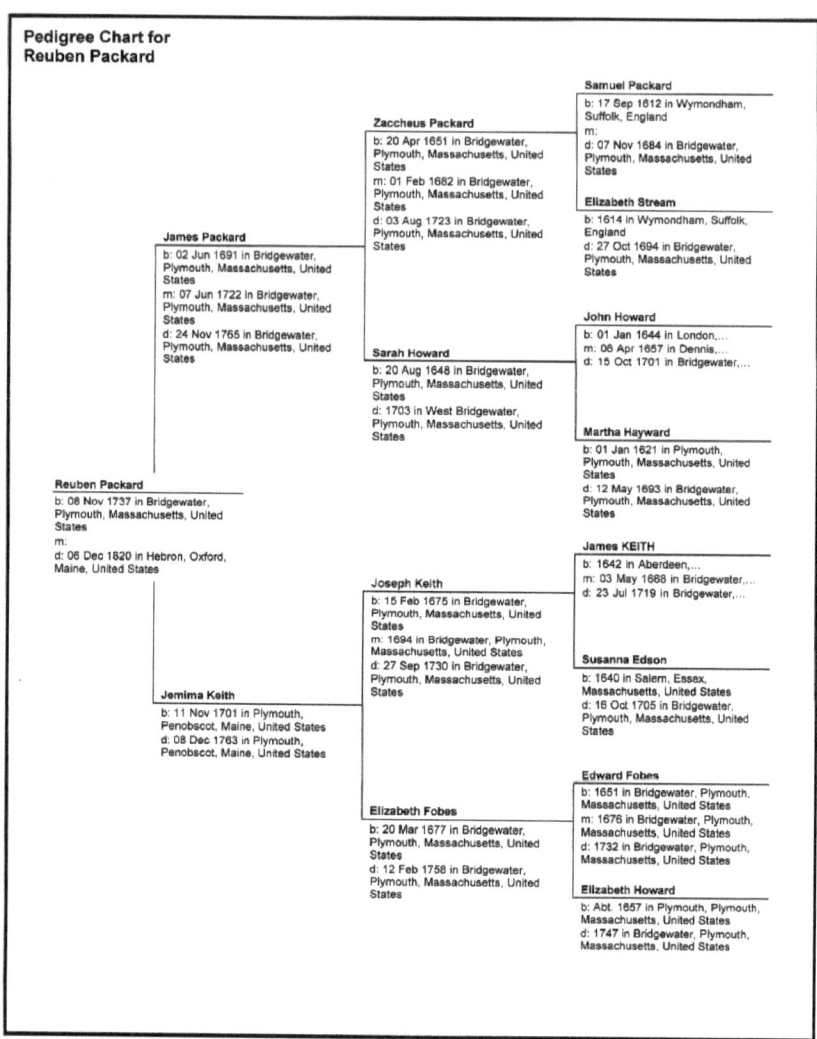

Pedigree Chart for Reuben Packard

Reuben Packard
b: 08 Nov 1737 in Bridgewater, Plymouth, Massachusetts, United States
m:
d: 06 Dec 1820 in Hebron, Oxford, Maine, United States

James Packard
b: 02 Jun 1691 in Bridgewater, Plymouth, Massachusetts, United States
m: 07 Jun 1722 in Bridgewater, Plymouth, Massachusetts, United States
d: 24 Nov 1765 in Bridgewater, Plymouth, Massachusetts, United States

Jemima Keith
b: 11 Nov 1701 in Plymouth, Penobscot, Maine, United States
d: 08 Dec 1763 in Plymouth, Penobscot, Maine, United States

Zaccheus Packard
b: 20 Apr 1651 in Bridgewater, Plymouth, Massachusetts, United States
m: 01 Feb 1682 in Bridgewater, Plymouth, Massachusetts, United States
d: 03 Aug 1723 in Bridgewater, Plymouth, Massachusetts, United States

Sarah Howard
b: 20 Aug 1648 in Bridgewater, Plymouth, Massachusetts, United States
d: 1703 in West Bridgewater, Plymouth, Massachusetts, United States

Joseph Keith
b: 15 Feb 1675 in Bridgewater, Plymouth, Massachusetts, United States
m: 1694 in Bridgewater, Plymouth, Massachusetts, United States
d: 27 Sep 1730 in Bridgewater, Plymouth, Massachusetts, United States

Elizabeth Fobes
b: 20 Mar 1677 in Bridgewater, Plymouth, Massachusetts, United States
d: 12 Feb 1758 in Bridgewater, Plymouth, Massachusetts, United States

Samuel Packard
b: 17 Sep 1612 in Wymondham, Suffolk, England
m:
d: 07 Nov 1684 in Bridgewater, Plymouth, Massachusetts, United States

Elizabeth Stream
b: 1614 in Wymondham, Suffolk, England
d: 27 Oct 1694 in Bridgewater, Plymouth, Massachusetts, United States

John Howard
b: 01 Jan 1644 in London,...
m: 06 Apr 1657 in Dennis,...
d: 15 Oct 1701 in Bridgewater,...

Martha Hayward
b: 01 Jan 1621 in Plymouth, Plymouth, Massachusetts, United States
d: 12 May 1693 in Bridgewater, Plymouth, Massachusetts, United States

James KEITH
b: 1642 in Aberdeen,...
m: 03 May 1668 in Bridgewater,...
d: 23 Jul 1719 in Bridgewater,...

Susanna Edson
b: 1640 in Salem, Essex, Massachusetts, United States
d: 16 Oct 1705 in Bridgewater, Plymouth, Massachusetts, United States

Edward Fobes
b: 1651 in Bridgewater, Plymouth, Massachusetts, United States
m: 1676 in Bridgewater, Plymouth, Massachusetts, United States
d: 1732 in Bridgewater, Plymouth, Massachusetts, United States

Elizabeth Howard
b: Abt. 1657 in Plymouth, Plymouth, Massachusetts, United States
d: 1747 in Bridgewater, Plymouth, Massachusetts, United States

My Common, Remarkable Family

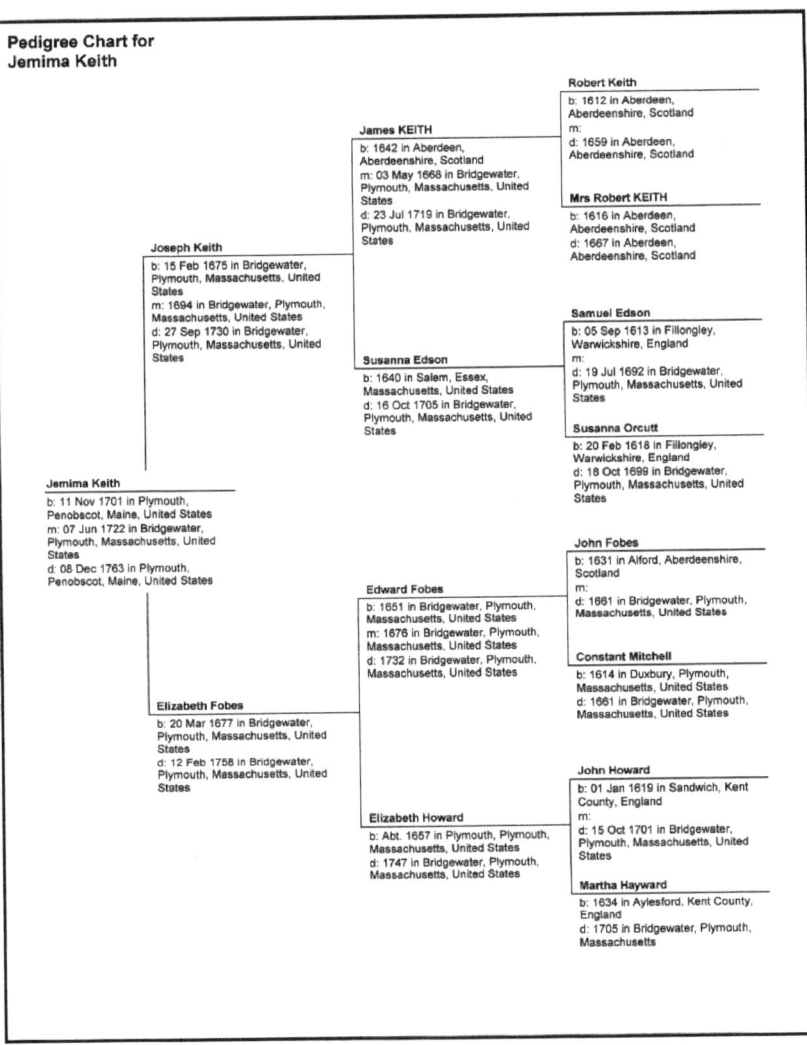

4. Best available genealogy for George Hadley Allen

Line includes early Virginia settlers including the Meriwether and Lewis families that included Meriwether Lewis of the Lewis and Clark Expedition. Includes possible link with the possible link to King George III and Hannah Lightfoot

My Common, Remarkable Family

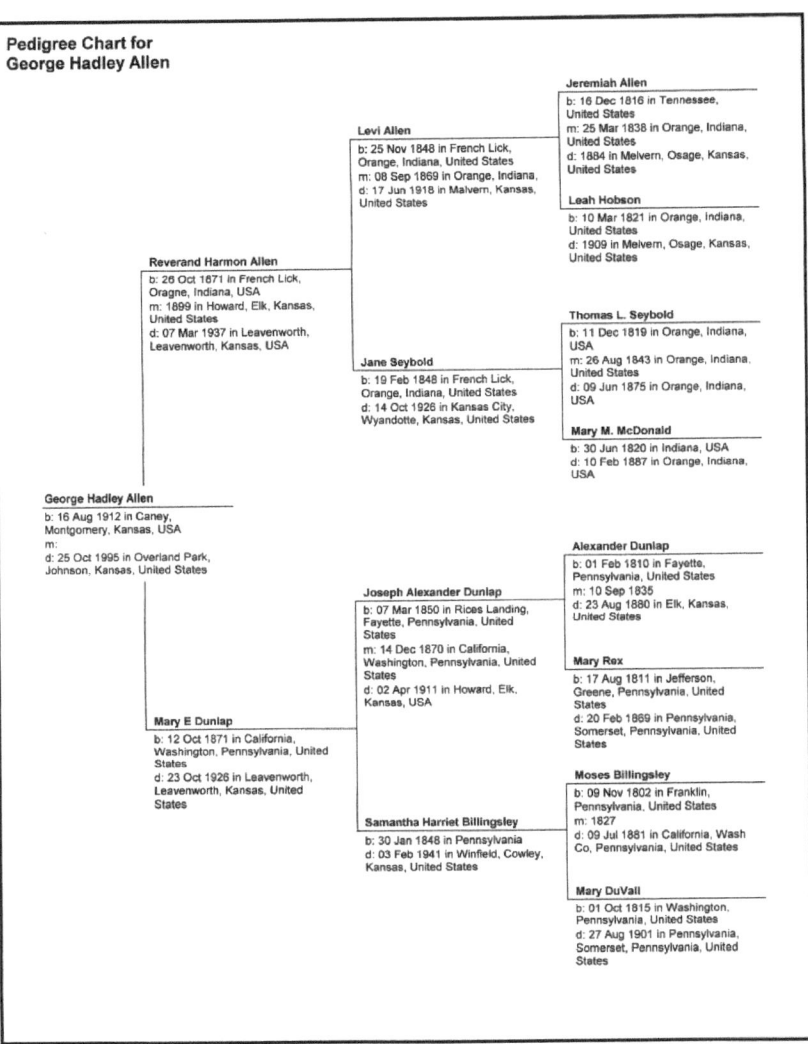

Tony Allen

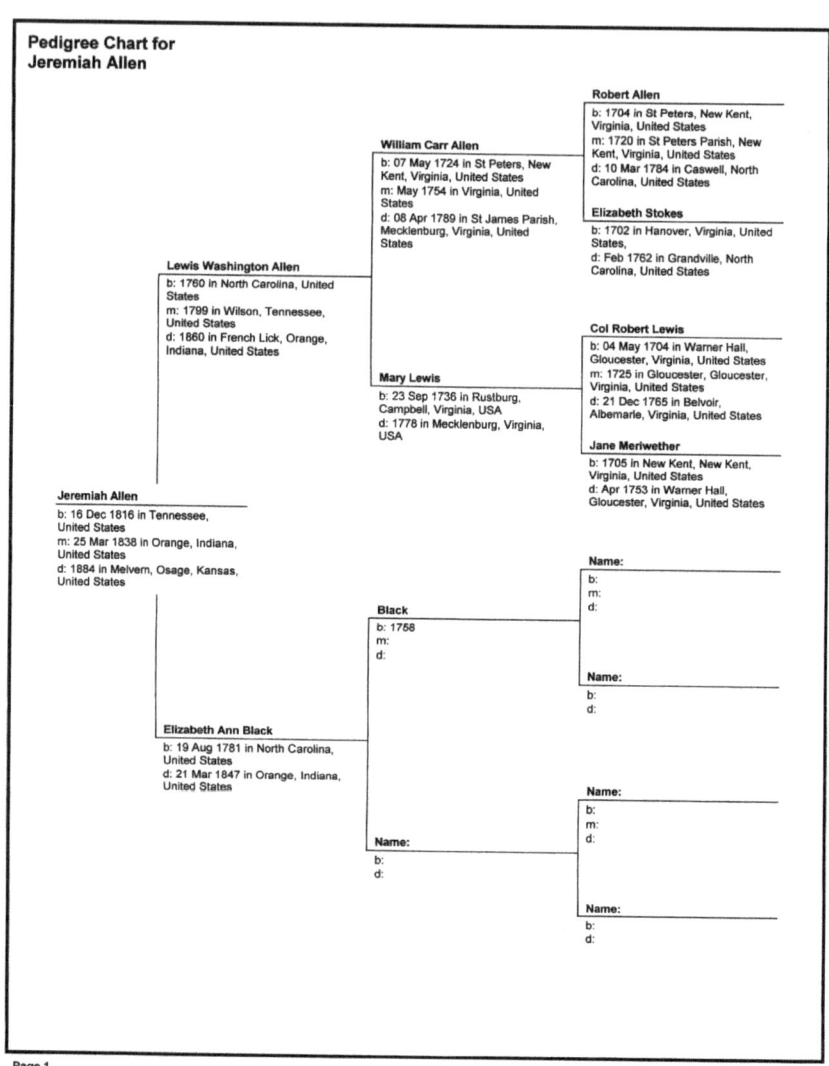

My Common, Remarkable Family

Pedigree Chart for Mary Lewis

- **Mary Lewis**
  - b: 23 Sep 1736 in Rustburg, Campbell, Virginia, USA
  - m: May 1754 in Virginia, United States
  - d: 1778 in Mecklenburg, Virginia, USA

- **Col Robert Lewis**
  - b: 04 May 1704 in Warner Hall, Gloucester, Virginia, United States
  - m: 1725 in Gloucester, Gloucester, Virginia, United States
  - d: 21 Dec 1765 in Belvoir, Albemarle, Virginia, United States

- **Col John Lewis**
  - b: 30 Nov 1669 in New Kent, New Kent, Virginia, United States
  - m: 1692 in Warner Hall, Gloucester, Virginia, United States
  - d: 14 Nov 1725 in Warner Hall, Gloucester, Virginia, United States

- **Elizabeth Warner**
  - b: 24 Nov 1672 in Warner Hall, Gloucester, Virginia, United States
  - d: 05 Feb 1720 in Warner Hall, Gloucester, Virginia, United States

- **John Lewis**
  - b: 1635 in Warner Hall, Gloucester, Virginia, United States
  - m:
  - d: 1689 in New Kent, New Kent, Virginia, United States

- **Isabella Miller**
  - b: 24 Aug 1640 in Warner Hall, Gloucester, Virginia, United States
  - d: 09 Feb 1704 in Petsworth Parish, Gloucester, Virginia, United States

- **Augustine Warner**
  - b: 03 Jun 1642 in Warner Hall, Gloucester, Virginia, United States
  - m:
  - d: 19 Jun 1681 in Warner Hall, Gloucester, Virginia, United States

- **Mildred Reade**
  - b: 02 Oct 1643 in Warner Hall, Gloucester, Virginia, United States
  - d: 20 Oct 1686 in Warner Hall, Gloucester, Virginia, United States

- **Jane Meriwether**
  - b: 1705 in New Kent, New Kent, Virginia, United States
  - d: Apr 1753 in Warner Hall, Gloucester, Virginia, United States

- **Nicholas Meriwether**
  - b: 26 Oct 1667 in Surry, Surry, Virginia, United States
  - m: 1688 in James River, Buckingham, Virginia, United States
  - d: 12 Dec 1744 in Goochland, Goochland, Virginia, United States

- **Elizabeth Crawford**
  - b: 1672 in New Kent, New Kent, Virginia, United States
  - d: 1762 in Fredricksville, Louisa, VA, USA,

- **Nicholas Meriwether**
  - b: 1631 in Bramber, Sussex, , England
  - m:
  - d: 15 Dec 1678 in Lynnhaven Parish, Prince William, Virginia, United States

- **Elizabeth Woodhouse**
  - b: 1633 in Lower, Norfolk, Virginia, United States
  - d: Jan 1680 in Virginia, United States

- **David Crawford**
  - b: 1625 in Kilbernie, Aryshire, , Scotland
  - m:
  - d: 1710 in New Kent, New Kent, Virginia, United States

- **Jane Crawford**
  - b: 1633 in Virginia, United States
  - d: 1710 in St Peters Parish, New Kent, Virginia, United States

Tony Allen

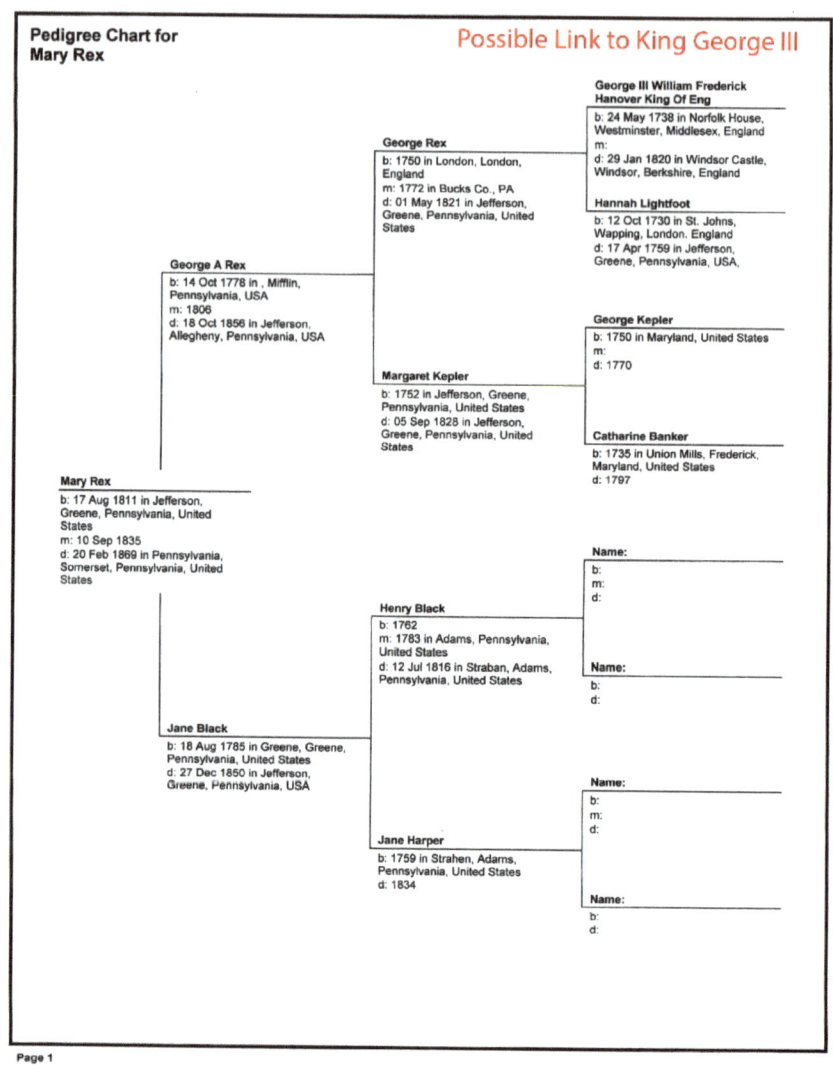

5. Handwritten letter by Georgiana to her Mother in Law

Bristo May 27 1877

Dear Mother
We havent heard from you since March. and would like to know how your health is this spring. We have been having two weeks of very wet weather so as to retard putting in the crops. The grasshoppers did not hatch out this spring here. George has rented out twenty acres of ground to put into corn. He will get half the crop in that feild. He will have nearly two acres of po- -tatoes and half an acre of sorghum beside garden vegetables He planted a bushel of Osage Orange seed on shares this year. He will have half the plants next spring We have all been to meeting today We go at nine in the morning to Sabbath school. and the Methodist preacher preaches afterwards. The children want me to tell you that they all got some very pretty chromos at S. S. to

The baby behaves very well in meeting. Samuels folks were there, and Josiah ford J is keeping school six or eight miles from here. She is called one of the best teachers about here. gets from 30 to 35 dollars a month. Sister Emma is keeping school at 32 dollars a month. She makes between 40 and 50 lbs of butter a week. nights and mornings. She makes the best butter of any body about here. Mother has not been quite so well lately. I am afraid she has too much work to do.

We think you have a very nice looking family of girls there. They must get a good education and come west as teachers. Teachers make the most money of any body in this country now.

Edith wants me to tell you that she is trying to get a prize that is offered in S. School. The Superintendent offers a pocket Bible to the scholar who repeats the most verses from the Bible.

George went to Mr Plummers to a toy-

rolling last night. They put up the logs to make a stable by moonlight. The farmers are all so busy now that he could not get any body in the daytime. Frank Jordans folks have a nice little boy about two months old.

I wish you could see our farm as it looks at this season of the year every thing is such a vivid green.

The children have bothered me so much that I could not write a good letter. Edith wanted to write a little to her cousin. I doubt if she will be able to read it. I hope you will encourage the children to write, for it is so much easier for them than for older people. We all send our love to you and all the rest of family.

   truly yours

    Georgiana Packard

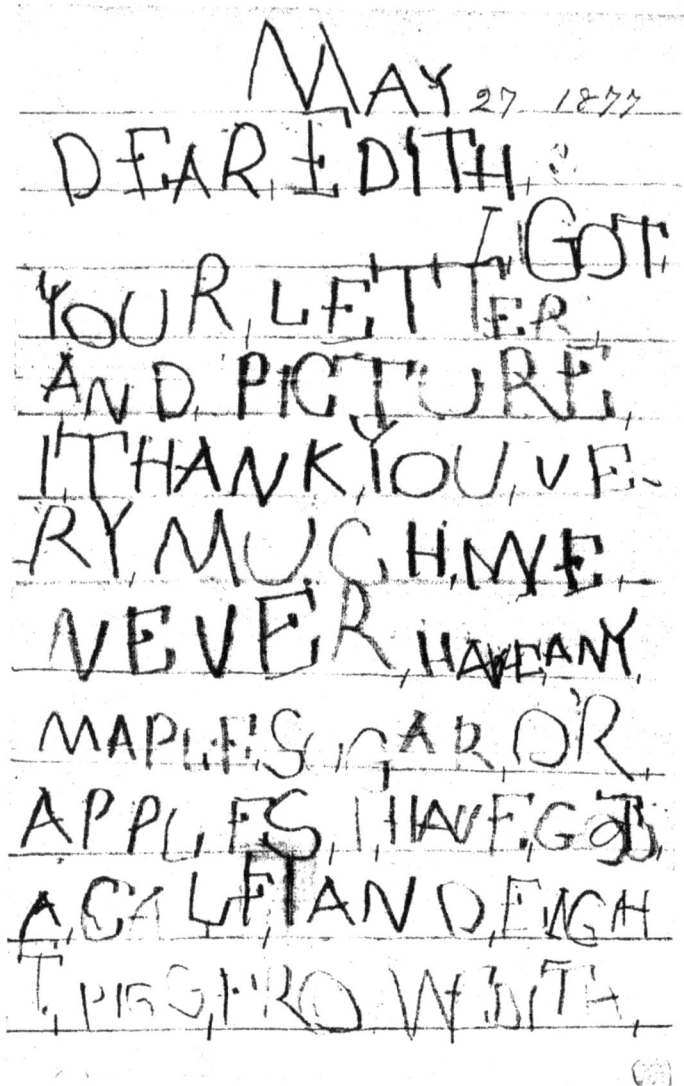

May 27 1877

Dear Edith,

I got your letter and picture, I thank you very much. We never have any maple sugar or apples. I have got a calf and eight pigs. Row with

6. Handwritten Letter by George Washington Packard

> Paola Kansas, May 7th 1863
>
> Dear Bro. Zibeon
>
> I received a letter from you last eave, and was very glad to hear from you, and to learn that you are yet alive, and well,
>
> You have sacrificed more than either of your brothers for your Country, for you had a wife, and little one too pan't with, wich no doubt was hard,
>
> I trust you will be rewarded for all you suffer, for your Country
>
> The indications are good for a spedy termination of the war,
>
> Gen. Herker is dooing well
>
> We shal hear favorably news soon from Vicksburg,
>
> The next attack on Charleston will result in the taking of it. (so says my best judgement)

The prospects for the success of our armes was never so flattering as at the presant time.

Starvation, grim starvation is now storing them in the face, and that is mans most terible enmy. Who can but pitty the poor women and inocent children, but it is none to good ber traitors.

Our reg. is stationed along the line to protect our our settlements from the bush wachers.

Murder, robery, and plunder seems to be the order of the day.

But the 7th Kansas is a terror to them. we are all well mounted and when we get on there trale our Goligers patent rifles, and Colts Dragoon revolvers are apt to talk in a thundering toune to them.

You can hardly immagin the amount of traviling I have done through the bush in Arkansas & Mo.

I wish I could talk to you all day.

I presume that you will have a chance to give the rebs, one or two shots before you go home, not that I am anxious to have you gett into dander, but conclude that you are anxious to do it.

We had a heavy frost here last night, it probably has done much damage, but think that we shal have a good "crop" season this year.

I intend to go home after the war is over, but it will not be the young "fop" that left there six years ago. The chang has been great probably on all of us.

I am a western man all over, but dont think that is an improvement by any means. Pleas direct Paola Co. A, 9th Reg. K.Vs. Paola Ks

With much love I close
                    Yours Truly
(Write soon)   Geo. W. Packard

7. George W. Packard Pay Records.

When we were visiting Ft. Pickens in Pensacola there was an advertisement for getting Civil War Pay records for veterans. I (Tony) applied for them and a couple of months later these showed up in the mail. They illustrate the life of a volunteer in the Kansas Cavalry who served as a Private during the Civil War.

My Common, Remarkable Family

P | 9 Cav. | Kans.

Geo. W. Packard
Lt., Co. D, 8 Reg't Kansas Vols *

Appears on

Company Muster Roll

for Nov & Dec, 1861.

Present or absent: Present
Stoppage, $........100 for ....
Due Gov't, $........100 for ....

Valuation of horse, $............100
Valuation of horse equipments, $............100
Remarks: ....

* This organization subsequently became Co. A, 9 Reg't Kans. Cav.

Book mark: ....

(358)   Copyist.

P | 9 Cav. | Kans.

Geo. W. Packard
Corpl., Co. D, 8 Reg't Kansas Vols *

Appears on

Company Muster Roll

for Jan & Feb, 1862.

Present or absent: Present
Stoppage, $........100 for ....
Due Gov't, $........100 for ....

Valuation of horse, $............100
Valuation of horse equipments, $............100
Remarks: Promoted from Prin
to Corpl Feb 1 '62.

* This organization subsequently became Co. A, 9 Reg't Kans. Cav.

Book mark: ....

(358)   Copyist.

Tony Allen

| P | 9 Cav. | Kans. |

Geo. W. Packard

Corpl., Co. A, 9 Reg't Kansas Cavalry.

Appears on

Company Muster Roll

for Mch & Apl, 1862.

Present or absent: present

Stoppage, $ 100 for

Due Gov't, $ 100 for

Valuation of horse, $ 100

Valuation of horse equipments, $ 100

Remarks: mustered in Sept. 13/61, at Ft. Leavnwth.

Book mark:

(358) Cardoze, Copyist.

| U | 9 Cav. | Kans. |

Geo. W. Packard

Pvt., Co. A, 9 Reg't Kansas Vols.*

Appears on

Company Muster Roll

for May & June, 1862.

Present or absent: present

Stoppage, $ 100 for

Due Gov't, $ 100 for

Valuation of horse, $ 100

Valuation of horse equipments, $ 100

Remarks:

*This organization subsequently became Co. A, 9 Reg't Kans. Cav.

Book mark:

(358) Cardoze, Copyist.

P | 9 Cav. | Kans.	P | 9 Cav. | Kans.
Geo. W. Packard	Geo. W. Packard
Corpl, Co. A, 9 Reg't Kansas Vols.*	Corpl, Co. A, 9 Reg't Kansas V
Appears on	Appears on
Company Muster Roll	**Company Muster Roll**
for July & Aug, 186 2	for Sep & Oct, 186 2
Present or absent... present	Present or absent... present
Stoppage, $......100 for.........	Stoppage, $......100 for.........
Due Gov't, $......100 for.........	Due Gov't, $......100 for.........
Valuation of horse, $......100	Valuation of horse, $......100
Valuation of horse equipments, $......100	Valuation of horse equipments, $......100
Remarks:	Remarks:
* This organization subsequently became Co. A, 9 Reg't Kans. Cav.	* This organization subsequently became Co. A, 9 Reg't Kans. Cav.
Book mark:	Book mark:
(358) Cardozo Copyist.	(358) Cardozo Copyist.

Tony Allen

| 9 Cav. | Kans.

Geo. W. Packard
Corpl., Co. A, 9 Reg't Kansas Cavalry.
Appears on
Company Muster Roll
for Nov. & Dec., 1862.
Present or absent Absent
Stoppage, $ 100 for
Due Gov't, $ 100 for
Valuation of horse, $ 100
Valuation of horse equipments, $ 100
Remarks: Detached acting orderly sergt of Co. B, 3rd Reg't Indian Home Guards.

Book mark:

Wheatly
Copyist.
(358)

| 9 Cav. | Kans.

George W. Packard
Corpl., Co. A, 9 Reg't Kansas Vols. Cav.
Appears on
Company Muster Roll
for Jan'y & Feb., 1863.
Present or absent Present
Stoppage, $ 100 for
Due Gov't, $ 100 for
Valuation of horse, $ 100
Valuation of horse equipments, $ 100
Remarks: Furnished horse and equipments from Nov. 5, 1862 to Feb. 28, 1863.

*This organization subsequently became Co. A, 9 Reg't Kans. Cav.

Book mark:

Wheatly
Copyist.
(358)

| P. | 9 Cav. | Kans.

George W. Packard
Corpl., Co. A, 9 Reg't Kansas Cavalry.
Appears on
Company Muster Roll
for March & April, 1863.
Present or absent Present
Stoppage, $ 100 for
Due Gov't, $ 100 for
Valuation of horse, $ 100
Valuation of horse equipments, $ 100
Remarks: Furnished horse & equipments from Feb 28 to April 30, 1863. Due U.S. for horse equipments $3.88

Book mark:

(358) Wheatly Copyist.

| P. | 9 Cav. | Kans.

George W. Packard
Corpl., Co. A, 9 Reg't Kansas Cavalry.
Appears on
Company Muster Roll
for May & June, 1863.
Present or absent Present
Stoppage, $ 100 for
Due Gov't, $ 100 for
Valuation of horse, $ 100
Valuation of horse equipments, $ 100
Remarks: Furnished horse & equipments from April 3 to June 30, 1863.

Book mark:

(358) Wheatly Copyist.

Tony Allen

| 1 | Cav. | Kans.

Geo. W. Packard

Sergt., Co. A, 9 Reg't Kansas Cavalry.

Appears on

Company Muster Roll

for .... July & Aug ...., 1863.

Present or absent .... Present ....

Stoppage, $........ 100 for ....

Due Gov't, $........ 100 for ....

Valuation of horse, $........ 100

Valuation of horse equipments, $........ 100

Remarks: Furnished horse & equipments from June 30 to Aug 31, 1863. Promoted from Corpl. July 19, 1863.

Book mark: ....

(858) .... Wheatly .... Copyist.

| 2 | 9 Cav. | Kans.

Geo. W. Packard

Sergt., Co. A, 9 Reg't Kansas Cavalry.

Appears on

Company Muster Roll

for .... Sept. & Oct ...., 1863.

Present or absent .... Present ....

Stoppage, $........ 100 for ....

Due Gov't, $........ 100 for ....

Valuation of horse, $........ 100

Valuation of horse equipments, $........ 100

Remarks: Furnished horse & equipments from Aug 31 to Oct 31, 1863.

Book mark: ....

(858) .... Wheatly .... Copyist.

| P | 9 Cav. | Kans.

George W. Packard
Pvt., Co. A, 9 Reg't Kansas Vols. Cav.

Appears on

Company Muster Roll

for .... Nov. & Dec. ...., 1863.

Present or absent .... Present ....

Stoppage, $ .... 100 for ....

Due Gov't, $ .... 100 for ....

Valuation of horse, $ 100

Valuation of horse equipments, $ 100

Remarks: Reduced to the Ranks from Sergt. Dec. 7, 1863. Furnished horse & equipments from Oct. 31 to Dec. 31, 1863.

Book mark: ....

Wheatly
(358) Copyist.

| C | 9 Cav. | Kans.

Geo. W. Packard
Pvt., Co. A, 9 Reg't Kansas Cavalry.

Appears on

Company Muster Roll

for .... Jan. Feb. ...., 1864.

Present or absent .... Present ....

Stoppage, $ .... 100 for ....

Due Gov't, $ .... 100 for ....

Valuation of horse, $ 100

Valuation of horse equipments, $ 100

Remarks: Furnished horse & equipments from Dec. 31, 63 to Feb. 29/64.

Book mark: ....

E N Brown
(358) Copyist.

| | 9 Cav. | Kans. |

George W Packard
Pvt, Co. A, 9 Reg't Kansas Cavalry.

Appears on
Company Muster Roll
for Mar & Apr, 1864.
Present or absent... Present
Stoppage, $ ___ 100/100 for ___
Due Gov't, $ ___ 100/100 for ___
Valuation of horse, $ ___ 100/100
Valuation of horse equipments, $ ___ 100/100
Remarks: Furnished horse & equipments from Feb 29/64 to Apl 29/64

Book mark: ___

(358)   E A H Brown
                    Copyist.

| | 9 Cav. | Kans. |

Geo. W. Packard
Pvt, Co. A, 9 Reg't Kansas Cavalry.

Appears on
Company Muster Roll
for May & June, 1864.
Present or absent... Present
Stoppage, $ ___ 100/100 for ___
Due Gov't, $ 1 90/100 for Ordnance
Valuation of horse, $ ___ 100/100
Valuation of horse equipments, $ ___ 100/100
Remarks: Furnished horse equipments from Feb 29/64 to June 30/64

Book mark: ___

(358)   E A H Brown
                    Copyist.

| C | 9 Cav. | Kans. |

George W. Packard

Pvt, Co. A, 9 Reg't Kansas Cavalry.

Appears on

Company Muster Roll

for July & Aug, 1864.

Present or absent .... Present

Stoppage, $ .... 100/100 for ....

Due Gov't, $ .... 1 40/100 for ord.

Valuation of horse, $ 100/100

Valuation of horse equipments, $ 100/100

Remarks: Furnished horse & equipments from Feb 29/64 to Aug 31/64.

Nxt borne on Co. M.O. Roll, Nov. 19/64.

Book mark: ....

E. N. Bunn
(358)   Copyist.

| C | 9 Cav. | Kans. |

George W. Packard

Cpl, Co. A, 9 Reg't Kansas Cavalry.

Age 28 years.

Appears on Co., **Muster-out Roll**, dated

Leavenworth, Kans., Nov. 19, 1864.

Muster-out to date Nov. 19, 1864.

Last paid to Feb. 29, 1864.

Clothing account:

Last settled Dec. 31, 1863; drawn since $ 100

Due soldier $ .... 100; due U.S. $ 100

Am't for cloth'g in kind or money adv'd $ 76 07/100

Due U.S. for arms, equipments, &c., $ 70/100

Bounty paid $ .... 100; due $ 100 100/100

Valuation of horse, $ 100

Valuation of horse equipments, $ 100

Remarks: Due U.S. for C & G E $2.21 Promoted from Private to Cpl Feb 1/62. Promoted Sgt July 1/63. Reduced to the ranks Dec 5/62 by order of Col Lynde 9 K.V.C. Furnished horse & equipm ents from ...... over.

Book mark: 1022 5-B-(E.B.)-75.

E. N. Bunn
(861)   Copyist.

Tony Allen

JUN 16 10382133

Feb. 29/64 to Sept. 7/64 Lost him in the service Sept. 7/64.

9 Cav. | Kansas.

Geo. W. Packard

Pvt., Co. A, 9 Reg't Kansas Cavalry.
Corp
Appears on Returns as follows:

Nov. 1861 (Ca - C. E. 8" K. M.)
absent on det.
service (as Police
Constable in
Shawnee Co.) from
Nov. 27. 1861 -
Nov. 1862. Absent on
det. ser. with 2"
Indian Regt. Home
Guards
Dec. 1862. Absent 1" Sgt.
Co. B 3 Indian Regt.
Apl. 1863 - Corp. Absent
Det - service
Dec. 1863. Pos. On daily
duty Ambulance
driver -
Jan. 1864 - On daily
duty Teamster.

also appears as E. W.
Book mark:

(546) Elliott Copyist.

ABOUT THE AUTHOR

None of the writers of this document could be construed as professional writers. Georgiana and George Washington Packard filled their days surviving as Pioneers on the Kansas Prairie and raising nine children. According to George Allen, Harmon excelled at oratory and ministry. Ruth and George Allen, besides raising four sons, made their careers in the Post Office and in secretarial work. Tony Allen, who edited this little volume trained as a scientist and most of his writing appears in technical literature. Nevertheless the family story shared in this book, while not atypical, is compelling as a snapshot of American History.

www.ingramcontent.com/pod-product-compliance
Lightning Source LLC
Chambersburg PA
CBHW041350290426
44108CB00001B/2